The Leopard That Changed Its Spots

Tim Haigh

Scripture quotations are taken from,

THE MESSAGE (bible) copyright 1993, 1994, 1995, 1996, 2000, 2001, 2002. Used by permission of NavPress publishing group.

Author's note
Out of consideration for friends and families I have,
in some instances, changed the names of persons In this book.

Edited by Stephen Matthew (www.stephenmatthew.com)

Cover design Tom Fernandez (thomas.b.fernandez@gmail.com)

Printed and bound by CPI Group (UK) Ltd, Croydon CR0 4YY

Tim Haigh publishers.

Contents

DEDICATION

This book is dedicated to all who have, and are currently suffering at the hands of addiction, in whatever the form it entered your world.

To every mother, father, spouse, partner, family member or friend, who has walked alongside, endured with, or lost a loved one through those circumstances, I honour you.

You may be down, but you are not out. Your heart may be bleeding, but it can be healed. You may not believe in yourself, but there is someone who believes in you wholeheartedly.

In Honour of my Mum and Dad

You gave me life, which now continues through me, my children and on into future generations.

Mum: you have always loved me unconditionally, even when I gave you none in return and I'm more grateful for it than you will ever know. You are always there when I need you and concerned for me even when I don't want you to be. Your strength and sheer determination to survive whatever life has thrown at you, is an outstanding quality that has and always will be a source of inspiration to me. I love you Mum.

Dad: it may have taken us a while to get to where we are today, but we got there in the end and what we have now is all I've ever wanted. The laughter, jokes and manly banter make me smile even when we are not together, and I admire you immensely. I'm proud of you Dad and I love you.

A happy ending is worth the journey.

The Why Behind This Book

IT'S dark out there.

Statistics show and most people simply know, that the dark effects of drug addiction, alcoholism and criminal behaviour are ravaging families, communities and society itself. The fruit is there for all to see: broken relationships, premature deaths, estranged parents, fear-filled senior citizens feeling trapped in their own homes and a generation of young adults who demand their rights but take no responsibility for others or their actions. The list goes on.

Society must move on, communities long to develop and families yearn to thrive, but their momentum is too often hindered by these negative things. Making progress feels like wading through murky pools of hopelessness rather than blazing a trail to a hope-filled future.

The darkness caused by crime and addiction angers me, maybe because I have been a part of it. But it certainly motivates me to want to push it back. But what do I have to offer?

So what can one man do?

Well, I once heard someone say: "Don't shout at the darkness, simply light a candle." And that is what I can do.

This book is about a candle in the darkness. It is my life story, written with openness and honesty for all to see. My hope is that the candle of my life and the light it shines will make a positive contribution towards driving back the darkness of brokenness, loneliness, addiction and pain from the hearts and minds of my fellow human beings. And I pray it inspires you to join me, because a myriad candles make a sun!

Just as the first light from the creation of the universe has never stopped moving forward, my prayer and earnest desire is that the light this book represents will never stop bringing hope to the hopeless, freedom to prisoners of addiction and be a key to unlocking the chains that hold people captive from reaching their full potential.

I chose to light a candle.

Tim Haigh

1

The Fight of My Life

HOLDING tightly to the brass rail of the dock, I pulled myself forward in an effort to get a better view of things. I nervously scanned the courtroom and was, for a moment, captivated by the sight of the British legal system busy at work before me. Barristers, court staff, legal personnel and journalists were all busying themselves in what seemed strangely like a theatrical performance.

The room itself was quite large and boldly impressive, with an institutional feel about it. Wood panelling adorned its walls and ornate plasterwork framed the lofty ceiling, while the air was filled with what can only be described as an old musty smell that seemed to permeate everything in the place.

The 'cast' down on the floor of the courtroom moved around slowly, yet assuredly, speaking in hushed tones in order to quietly observe the etiquette of their surroundings. The Barristers, in their black gowns and white wigs, sat behind tables piled high with stacks of paperwork, and just in front of them sat the Court Clerk. Above them all sat the Judge, looking far too serious and stern I thought, observing everything yet talking to no one. Then, over to one side, I spotted the journalists, with pen and paper at the ready but looking rather bored.

I briefly glanced over my shoulder towards the public gallery. There sat some familiar faces; a group of friends and family in amongst others I'd never seen before in my life. I caught sight of mum and my heart warmed momentarily. So I gave her a quick smile and mouthed the words, "are you OK?"

She nodded and flashed me a false smile in return. I looked away again.

There were actually eight of us sat in the dock, plus two burly prison screws that meant we were tightly packed in. Two other guards were standing just outside the dock, talking to each other but never taking their eyes off us. In any other setting we would have looked like a normal bunch of teenagers; laughing, joking, poking each other and acting a little immaturely if I'm honest. But this was no normal everyday setting; we were in a Crown Court dock, about to be sentenced by that stern looking Judge, who was perched high above us on his throne-like chair adorned in his red cloak and white wig. This was serious.

How on earth had a bunch of teenagers like us ended up here?

Throughout the proceedings, I had joined in the smattering of smirks, sniggers and childish banter between us, as the severity of my actions had just not registered in my thinking. Then the mood changed. The hush of the courtroom was broken by the sound of the Judge's voice. He looked me squarely in the eyes and ordered me to stand to my feet. The journalists suddenly lost their bored expressions and looked alert with pens poised. The room fell silent, broken only by the muffled sound of traffic on the streets outside.

I took a deep breath and pulled myself to my feet using

the brass rail. I stood there, with my hands behind my back, trying to look as remorseful as I could as I tentatively engaged the Judge's stare. Inside, I was shaking like a leaf.

"Timothy John Haigh, I find you to be an aggressive and very violent young man. You have attacked three men, in an unprovoked and violent manner, leaving two of the defendants hospitalised, one of them in a coma fighting for his life. It was a grievous and totally unprovoked attack for which you are responsible. I have no doubt in my mind that you are the ringleader of this gang and as such, the sentence you are to receive will be the maximum I can give within sentencing guidelines. I take into account that you were only sixteen at the time of the offence; had you been older, the sentence imposed would have been significantly longer."

The Judge continued:

"For the Section 18 charge of wounding with intent, I sentence you to 3 years imprisonment. For the section 20 charge of Grievous Bodily Harm with intent, I sentence you to 2 years imprisonment. For the charge of violent disorder, I sentence you to 3 years imprisonment. For the charge of burglary of a dwelling, I sentence you to 9 months imprisonment. For the charge of burglary, I sentence you to 6 months imprisonment. For the additional 103 (one hundred and three) offences of burglary that are also to be taken into account, I sentence you to 6 months imprisonment. All these sentences ..."

I had stopped listening. All I heard was - take him down.

I was stunned. I felt numb and frozen to the spot. I just stood there in a daze, unable to comprehend what had just happened. I didn't move.

I was jolted back to reality by a strong hand taking me

by the upper arm and almost lifting me across the floor of the dock to the top of the steep stairs that led down to the cells below. In one well-rehearsed move the 'screw' marshalled me down into the cells without ever once releasing his grip on my arm. He marched me along a corridor, past cell door after cell door until we reached the end of the block where a solitary cell door stood open and I was pushed firmly inside. Before I had a chance to say a word, the heavy iron door was slammed shut behind me with a loud thud. I heard the jingle of keys as the lock was engaged and then listened as the screw walked away, his footsteps echoing on the hard floor until they eventually disappeared into the distance. Then, just silence.

I just stood there, letting my eyes adjust to the dim light for a couple of moments. It was hostile, silent and empty, except for a wooden bench at its far end. Eventually, I spun around and sat down on it, facing the door. As I surveyed the bare concrete cage that surrounded me, an overwhelming sense of isolation came over me; the reality of my situation hit me suddenly like a flood and I was devastated. All I could do was stare at the big iron door opposite me. It was my oppressor, my captor, my jailer. I just stared at it.

The deafening silence was only broken by the noise of my thoughts kicking in. What had just happened up there? I leaned forward and put my head in my hands, looking at the floor. I tried hard to remember what the steely-eyed Judge had said. "Timothy John Haigh …" his voice boomed in my head. "I sentence you to 3 years, 2 years, 3 years …" and how many months I pondered? I jolted upright and stood up. As I paced up and down the cell I began to panic. How long had I actually got? How

4

long was I going to be in prison? This wasn't how it was supposed to happen!

I tried to focus on something else, anything else, just to get the sound of his voice out of my head. My mind drifted back to my school days, not too many months earlier. I was young, carefree and energetic. How on earth had I ended up in this mess and in this cell today? Full of questions and short of answers in that sparsely lit prison cell, I said to myself, "This is the worst day of my life. My life can't get any worse than this!"

But I was mistaken. My life could get worse, much worse.

The battle begins

How had a young man, with so much promise ended up in that prison cell?

It all began seventeen years earlier, on what was for me a momentous day, the day my name was written into history, the day I was born! I'm told it was a bright, warm summer's evening when I arrived into this world on the fifteenth of July 1971, weighing in at 7lb 6oz. I was born with blue eyes – which I've kept – and had a fine head of wispy blonde hair, which didn't stay that colour for long. Mum was a fiery redhead and out of all of my siblings, I was the one who inherited her hair colour. There were no complications, so after a couple of days on the maternity ward, I was taken home to join my mum and dad and older brother.

I had only been home for ten days, when I was taken very ill and rushed back into hospital with gastroenteritis. It was serious. Back in the early seventies, the medicines we enjoy today were not as readily available and it was a condition that could easily kill a baby as young as I was. So I was quarantined with immediate effect. Mum wasn't allowed to touch or hold me and I was placed in a little bed surrounded by a clear plastic tent to prevent the spread of my sickness, cut off from my loved ones. Things worsened, despite the best efforts of the doctors, and after two days of deterioration the doctors genuinely thought I was beyond recovery and feared the worst. They called in the hospital chaplain who, on the advice of the doctors, asked mum if he could give me the 'last rites' in preparation for a likely death.

Mum told him in no uncertain terms where he could stick his 'last rites' because her boy was not going to die, and that he had better get out of the room! I'm told the nurses in the room didn't know where to look, caught between the raw emotion of a mother's love and the medical reality they were dealing with. The Chaplain left the room very quietly and closed the door behind him.

Mum just sat there in the corner of the room and prayed for me; sat and prayed for her baby in the plastic tent that she longed to hold again. She was willing me to fight and live. Mum slept in a hospital side room each night and then came back into my room, all gowned up with mask and hat and gloves, as soon as she woke up. And there she would stay until exhaustion forced her to go and get the sleep she needed for the next day.

Day after day, mum sat alone in the corner of my room, praying quietly as the doctors and nurses medicated my limp body. Words of comfort were offered, but we now know that the doctors actually held little hope of recovery for me. It was as if death itself was battling to have me, to snatch my young life away before it had hardly begun. I was of course oblivious to all this but have since talked about it with mum and frequently pondered the question, 'who was my defender?' Mum's prayers were certainly in the front line of the battle and I do believe that God wanted me to live, not die.

And I did – live, that is. After a week of being seemingly lifeless, I suddenly began to recover and the doctors were astounded by my rate of recovery. Little by little the activity in the room increased and mum, who had remained seated in the corner watching things unfold, now had genuine hope in her heart. She knew I was going to make it and all she now wanted to do was hold me and that's all she did, every waking hour that the doctors allowed her to remain at my bedside. Her prayers had been answered and after over two weeks of waiting, she took me home again.

That battle with death had been successful; we had won, but it wouldn't be the last time a battle for my life would rage around me.

Grandstand Road

Mum and dad were married in early 1970 and my older brother, Johnny, was born not too long after they tied the knot. They couldn't afford a home of their own, so they moved in with my nana Nellie - my dad's mum. She lived alone in a little village called Wrenthorpe, in the suburbs of Wakefield, West Yorkshire, where they settled down into family life with nana as a constant source of help and support.

That was to be the world I arrived into, but everything was not as it seemed on the surface. Dad was a young and undisciplined man who would frequently live his life as if he was still single. He would go out drinking with his mates whenever he felt like it and return at all hours. Mum would then have a go at him, demanding he took his responsibilities as a husband and father more seriously. He wouldn't listen and, come the next weekend, he would be off again until he decided to come home. In the end, it led to some furious bust ups between them, often getting violent, and nana would have to step in and restore the peace.

Over time it got worse; his aggressive behaviour becoming more frequent and physical until they started really hurting each other. She would confront him only to be pushed and slapped, then she would hit back. A full on fight would start and mum always tried to give as good as she got, but dad was stronger and she would end up sobbing in a pile on the floor, nursing her wounds and saying she hated him. Nana always tried to stop these fights before they went too far but because her first priority was to make sure my brother was out of the way first, she didn't always make it. Afterwards they both would promise to stop behaving like this in nana's house and to be more considerate of their child. But it continued, and was the normal pattern of behaviour behind our closed doors when I arrived home from hospital to join the clan.

This stuff wasn't new to nana. She too had endured a marriage full of fights, violence and aggression. So, she would often sit with mum and encourage her to leave my dad. She hated to see them both fighting and feared that it would only get more extreme as time went on. Her advice was to get out whilst she could and protect herself and us kids from the violence.

I was three months old when she finally found the courage to leave him. It was after a particularly bad beating from dad and she had simply had enough. She secretly went to the Social Services for help and they found her some emergency accommodation with a caring and loving couple who had no children of their own. They lived in a house that had enough room to accommodate us all on the outskirts of Wakefield, so mum returned home and as soon as dad went out, she packed all our belongings and the three of us made the bus journey across town to our new home.

We lived with that lovely couple for about three months while the Social Services found us a home. When eventually one was found, they also helped us with all the arrangements to make the move to our new house as stress free as possible. And that's how we ended up in the village of Outwood, at number 3, Grandstand Road.

It was now 1972. Our new home was the third one along, in a row of fifteen one-up, one-down red brick terraced houses, built in the late 1800's. The houses sat at the side of an old dirt track, about four hundred yards from the main road, with fields to the rear and sides. The accommodation consisted of one big room on the ground floor that had a kitchen area at one end, a coal fire in the middle of the side wall – which was the only source of heating and hot water in the house – and an area under the front window where we used to sit and eat. Upstairs was one big room too, with one window on the front wall and a small one on the back wall. That was it.

There was no indoor toilet, as was common for houses built that long ago. Instead they were housed in a red brick block, just around the back of the row. It contained five toilets, which served all fifteen houses – hardly private. The only thing that separated you from everyone else was a rickety old door that was so ill fitting a small person could climb under the gap at the bottom of it!

When it came to bath time, in the early days mum would warm pans of water up on the coal fire and fill the kitchen sink for us to happily splash around in. Then as we got bigger, she got an old tin bath that was put in front of the fire and filled with hot water. Johnny and I would get in together, one at each end – good for splashing each other – as mum attempted to clean us up.

Back together

Dad eventually got to know where we were living and came around to see mum. After a lot of persuasion and promises, she let him move back in and the family unit was intact again. She had her reasons for making that decision and, as ever, she did what she thought was best for us all. Within weeks of dad moving back in, mum fell pregnant and my younger brother Terry was born in the January of the following year, 1973.

Life on Grandstand Road was a typical seventies existence – if you are from that era you will know what I mean! The neighbouring families were a mixed bunch, most of them had kids like us, then there were a few middle-aged couples whose kids had grown up and a couple of very old people. Our next-door neighbours to one side were a Scottish couple called Jimmy and Margaret. Margaret became like another mum to us, often baby sitting and cooking little treats for us. Jimmy was a true Scotsman, who I could barely understand because of his accent, which apparently was not a bad thing as mum said he swore every time he opened his mouth. He would spend hours sitting and playing with us in the street, always dressed in the same thick trousers and waist coat, whilst smoking one of his skinny little roll ups. I got to know some of his swear words and much to mum's embarrassment would trot them out when we were on the bus or in other public places. Like all kids, I just copied what I saw and heard.

On the other side lived a single mum called Andrea who had a son called David, who was a little older than my brother Johnny. He played out with us all day long. When us street kids played out, we would all share whatever toys we had – which led to a lot of arguments – but we never tired of running around together playing in the muck or kicking a ball about. There was always an adult sat out in front of one of the houses, simply watching out for the other mums and dads. It felt like one small, tight-knit family community.

Terry, my younger brother seemed to grow fast and was soon wanting to be out with us older kids in the street. He would try to join in with our games but we were having none of it. We would run away and he could never catch us because he still wore those terry-towelling nappies – this was long before disposables were invented! Some days he would run around outside with no trousers on and his nappy would be so saturated, it sagged down past his knees, making it hard for him to walk so he would just waddle around like a duck. We thought it was hilarious! Mum would eventually spot him and sort him out, but boy, those nappies used to stink the house out when mum soaked and cleaned them; the smells of childhood!

Ouch!

By the time Johnny was getting on for five, he was growing ganglier each day. He also had big 'sticky out' front teeth that he hated. But I had my own burden to bear - my ginger hair was getting brighter and brighter. It was very red and wiry with a style all of its own - none! I wasn't too self-conscious about it in those early years but that would change in the years to come.

One night, long after we had gone to bed, us kids were woken by the sound of ambulance sirens outside the house. We jumped out of bed and looked out of the window, only to be dazzled by the blue flashing lights. Then we saw a growing crowd of our neighbours gathered outside, so we crept downstairs out of sheer curiosity. We were greeted by the sight of my dad sat on the sofa with a blood-soaked towel wrapped around his hand. Other blood stained cloths lay around on the floor by his feet. Two ambulance men were quizzing him about where his injury was – it didn't take a lot to work that one out Sherlock! Then they took off the towel to see the extent of his injuries and blood spurted out from two stumps that used to be fingers on his right hand. Blood went everywhere and he was quickly moved to the ambulance for further treatment and then taken to hospital. Suddenly mum caught sight of us on the stairs and ushered us back up to bed and that was that.

The story went that he had fallen whilst walking along the side of the railway line, close to where we lived. He was drunk of course. So as he attempted to get back up in his drunken stupor, he had grabbed hold of the train track to steady himself, not noticing a train was about to drive past him. It ran over the two fingers he had on the track and crushed them to flaps of skin. It could so easily have killed him.

It is funny how people like my family think about things like this. Believe it or not, my dad reckoned he was better off after the accident than before it with all his fingers! Basically his benefits changed from 'looking for work' dole, to disability benefits because he was deemed unfit to work. This meant more money and he didn't have to go to the dole office to be taught how to look for work which was a good outcome in his mind.

So that was our family life. We were scruffy little kids with snotty noses, playing out in all weathers without a care in the world and living from 'giro' to 'giro' on government benefits.

The visitor

One day, when Jonny was five and I was coming up to four, we made a discovery: we found a small gap in the fence opposite our house. It was right at the end where the fence met an old brick wall to which it was supposed to be securely fixed. But it wasn't. Curiosity drove us through the hole in the fence, Johnny leading the way and me happily following. We entered a strange new place, the rear yard of the food factory that was opposite our houses. As we explored our newfound playground, we came across two strange looking buildings that we couldn't find a way round. We both looked up at the same time to discover that the strange buildings blocking our path rose high into the sky: in fact they were two very tall towers.

We were too young to know that they were powder silos that held the ground wheat used for making bread and pastries. The slightly smaller one was at least sixty feet tall and the one next to it was a good ten feet taller.

As we gazed up at the two strange towers, our eyes fell on the access ladder that ran up the side of the smaller one. A new challenge! Johnny started to climb and I followed. Up we went, blissfully unaware of the potential dangers.

Meanwhile, mum was in the house cleaning and minding her own business when she heard a knock at the door. She stopped what she was doing, opened the door and was surprised to see an elderly gentleman standing there. He had white hair and wore a smart shiny grey suit, crisp white shirt and a necktie to complete his outfit. He had a kind and warm face.

"I'm so sorry to disturb you", he said, "but I was wondering if you could please spare me a glass of water?"

This was unusual; she'd certainly never seen him before and he looked a bit out of place in Grandstand Road. Nevertheless, she agreed.

"Of course" she said. She walked across the room to the kitchen area, got a glass, making sure it was clean first and filled it with cold water. She passed him the glass and he took it with a smile, raised it to his mouth began to slowly drink the water. Meanwhile, mum looked on inquisitively. He didn't alarm her, she was just curious to know who he was and what was he doing on Grandstand Road. It just wasn't the sort of road people walked down because it led to nowhere.

After finishing his water, the gentleman handed the glass back to mum with a warm smile and a kindly, "thank you so much".

She just smiled back, albeit quizzically, as it was all still a bit odd.

"You're welcome", she finally responded as she reached to close the door, thinking it was all over, when he said,

"I would just like to say that everything is going to work out fine for you".

Mum stopped dead. She looked at him intently, impacted by his calming voice and a strange feeling that he knew something she didn't.

He continued, "You have wonderful children and I want you to know that your children will be fine. Everything will turn out just fine". And with that he smiled, thanked her again for the water, turned and began to walk away.

She left the door open and turned back into the house to put the glass in the sink, thinking about what he had said: "You have wonderful children ... Your children will be fine". Then the thought hit her, "Where are my kids?"

She hurried through the open door and looked left and right up and down the street to see where we were. But we were nowhere to be seen, so she shouted for us. Nothing. Then she noticed that she couldn't see the old gentleman either. He'd only been gone a few seconds before she rushed out to find us. Where had he gone? There was no sign of him or the kids; she was perplexed.

She shouted again. Still nothing. Then she saw Margaret, our neighbour, stood on her front doorstep smoking a cigarette.

"Have you seen an old man just walk past?" She asked her.

"No love", responded Margaret, "Why?"

"Oh nothing", mum said half heartedly, her thoughts still trying to make sense of it all. He was nowhere to be seen.

Again she scanned the street for us and then the field

behind the house – nothing. Where were those kids? Then her gaze was drawn upwards and she froze with fear; she saw us almost at the top of the ladder on the side of the silo tower in the factory compound opposite the house. Panic-stricken, she shouted for Johnny as she and Margaret ran over the road to try and get to us. But the fence we had wriggled through blocked them, so they couldn't get near us.

By then Johnny and I were on top of the silos, without a care in the world and oblivious to the danger we were in. Once we reached the top of the ladder, there was no protective railing around the top of the silo. In the middle of the top was a hatch that was open. I walked over and peered in. It was full of ground floor, maybe two thirds full. Then I looked up and saw my brother climbing up a smaller ladder that led to the top of the higher tower. He reached the top and climbed on to that roof. Only then did I look around and realise how high up we were. I started to panic a little. Johnny had moved across the higher roof now and I couldn't see him. I looked into the hatch again and was mesmerised as I gazed in.

It was then that I heard my mum's voice, "Tim, Tim". I tried to look for her but couldn't see her anywhere. I stood still, frozen to the spot. Then a head came into sight at the top of the ladder, which startled me a little, and a reassuring face greeted me. I was gently coaxed over to the ladder by a caring and brave worker from the factory and helped back down to the safety of the ground. Johnny was brought down the same way too.

While this was going on, mum was still stuck behind the fence on our street. It transpired that a factory worker had heard her shouts, looked around and seen us at the top of the silo and raised the alarm. Once we were safely back down, mum rushed around the bottom road to the factory's main entrance to be reunited with us. What a relief! Lots of hugs and tears followed – as well as a stern telling off. Then to add a final bit of drama a fire engine turned up, followed by a police car, both called by someone at the factory. Fortunately, they were not needed, but it did all mean that the factory had to overhaul their safety features, fit new safety barriers around the top of the silos and make it harder to get on to the ladder. And of course our entry point through the fence was repaired too!

In spite of the drama it caused, Johnny and I were still a bit bemused by it all and thought that the whole thing had just been a bit of harmless fun.

So, what about the old gentleman? Where did he come from and where did he go? To this day, mum is convinced he was a guardian angel. If it were not for his turning up at the door exactly at the time he did, and the words he said, she wouldn't have been so intent on finding us. Her shouts wouldn't have alerted the factory worker who saw us and raised the alarm, and my life could have had a very different outcome. It seems he came from nowhere and returned to nowhere. I wonder? Whatever the case, I now feel like another battle for my life was won that day.

Moving on

The houses on Grandstand Road were fast becoming unfit for human habitation. Dampness was the biggest problem, which rose up from the ground and through the walls into the house. Even the carpet became damp in places and mould became an increasing problem on the walls.

Eventually it affected our health. Little coughs and colds became lingering chest infections so the family doctor wrote to the council on our behalf and an inspector came to examine the house. It turned out the whole row was suffering, so the council decided to re-house all the tenants and pull down the houses.

We knew that nothing would happen very quickly. But that winter of 1975 was a particularly cold and damp one. Our health suffered badly for months on end. Johnny's asthma flared up so badly that he spent weeks being treated in hospital and wasn't allowed home until the weather warmed up in the spring. Because of this, we were moved to the top of the relocation list and it just became a waiting game before we found out where we would be living next.

2

Future-Forming Forces

I REMEMBER moving in to our lovely new council house like it was yesterday.

Mum and dad had been talking about it for weeks and at long last the day arrived. We were moving into a modern home and couldn't wait to get there! My uncle Frank came with his flat-back pick-up truck to move our few items of furniture and other possessions the mile or so to Charles Avenue, a small cul-de-sac on the edge of a post-war council estate. Number 8 was a red brick semi-detached house with red clay roof tiles and metal-framed windows. The front garden was a decent size and a path ran down the side of the house to a very long back garden, maybe thirty or so meters long.

The first thing that struck me about the house was its bright green front door – you just couldn't miss it. Apparently it was just one of the vast number of council house door colours: red, yellow, blue or, you guessed it, bright green. That door remained the same shade of green for the next 25 years, and more, until it was changed to a white PVC plastic one. But I digress ... back to my childhood.

We kids – Johnny now six, Terry three and me four – pulled up outside the house and were lifted out of the back of the flat-back by our dad. He had been sitting in the back with us, nestled between the furniture, boxes and bags of clothes. We ran into the front garden, while he and uncle Frank began unloading the van. We had never had a front lawn before; I remember it feeling soft under our feet. It didn't hold our attention for too long because mum opened the front door and we all rushed to squeeze past her, eager to explore our new abode. The sound of our voices and the stomping of tiny feet echoed around the empty house. We explored the bedrooms then stopped briefly to marvel at the indoor toilet. Wow! This was a luxury compared to our old house. Back downstairs we ran and out of the back door – yes, we had two doors, another novelty – and into the back garden. It was big when compared to the average back yard but we weren't really that impressed because our old house had a field behind it that was the size of four football pitches and we counted that as our back garden.

I even remember our first meal there: sausage sandwiches in white bread – yummy! Not the brown bread my wife insists we eat now, full of seeds that get stuck in my teeth. Real white bread. We sat on the kitchen floor and gobbled our sandwiches down with our grubby hands, trying to eat as fast as we could so that we could get back to playing outside.

It was the start of a new season for our family; we had a house with all mod cons, including a separate kitchen and living room, indoor toilet, separate bathroom, three bedrooms and a safe garden. There was a coal fire in both of the downstairs rooms, which heated the house and our water via a back boiler. It was like a palace to us, when compared to the house we had just left.

I was soon to start Infant School, which meant mum

would only have Terry at home during the day. But that soon changed as she became pregnant with my new younger brother Jeremy. He was born in the spring of 1976 and the stench of smelly Terry-towelling nappies once more filled the house. Things were on the up for the Haigh family; or so it seemed.

I have vague but happy memories of that time. One is of walking Johnny to school with mum pushing Terry in his pram while she was heavily pregnant. I can picture the walk even now: up to the top of our cul-de-sac, across George Street into Andrew Crescent where we walked past more houses with bright green, blue, red or yellow front doors. Then we went round a bend, up the ginnel, crossed over Church Lane and up Monk Wood Crescent – this was a private estate where mum would say all the rich people lived. Then it was through another ginnel onto Ledger Lane where we turned left and walked past the park and the workingmen's club, eventually arriving at school. It's probably no more than half a mile but to my teeny legs, it seemed to be the longest walk in the world.

We had an old TV that sat on a large wooden cupboard in the corner of the room. It was a big old lump of a thing with large sticky-out buttons that you had to push to turn the channel over. They were so stiff that I had to use the strength of both my hands to push the button in far enough to turn over the channel. 'Clunk' would be the sound it made as the button sprang back out – no remotes in those days! We watched Pipkins, Mr Ben, the Flumps, the Wombles and Captain Pugwash. Happy days! They came on just after lunch each day and we never missed them. Mum would shout, "your programmes are on" and we would drop everything and plonk ourselves down in front of the 'goggle box' and enjoy our TV time. Back then, kids TV wasn't available all day long like it is today, so we just maximised the moment, then it was back outside to play.

Life was simple and carefree, as it is for most kids at that age: play, eat, sleep and start again the next day. Wonderful.

I also remember the times we would walk up to the community Health Centre, which happened weekly, to let the nurse have a look at us. Well, that's what mum told us we were going for. It sounded a bit strange but what did we care? and we always came away with our free milk tokens, which were given to families on benefits back in those days. I remember the milk tokens in particular, because out of all of the things our economic situation forced us to cut back on, milk was the one thing I hated being cut. You see, the benefits we received because dad couldn't or wouldn't work, didn't go very far, especially as mum and dad both smoked and loved a drink. Of course, it was never supposed to be used on those things, it was provided for essentials. But booze and 'ciggies' were treated as essentials in our house, so there had to be cutbacks in other areas and milk was one of them. Mum would therefore buy sterilised milk and then water it down to make it go further; making what seemed like five pints of watered down stuff from one pint bottle! It was like whitewash and I hated it with a passion; it was horrendous. It not only tasted disgusting, it made everything it was served with taste just as bad. Yuck! Even today, I still can't stand the thought of it.

Generational influences

On the surface, I reckon we looked like a pretty normal

council estate family, many of whom lived on benefits of various kinds like we did. But just beneath the surface, things were not so good. I really do wish I could tell you about my amazing parents who gave us kids everything we needed to equip us for success in life, but I can't. Having said that, I do know without question that mum and dad loved me and would certainly have laid down their lives for me. But I never wanted them to die for me, I wanted them to live for me and be a positive role model for me. Yet generational influences somehow made that a distant dream.

By this time, my dad would have been in his early twenties and hadn't had a job since leaving school. The 'train track' accident a few years earlier had, of course, contributed to that situation!

His upbringing was a mixed bag. His father, my granddad Frank, was a big man who stood over six feet tall and had red hair in the days before he started to go bald. Apparently, he had enjoyed some financial stability and had inherited quite a bit of money from his dad back in the fifties. So my dad wanted for nothing whilst growing up with his three older sisters and brother. In fact, it is said that he was spoilt. However, granddad Frank liked a drink, and when he was drunk – which increased over the years – he would have furious bust-ups with nana and be physically violent towards her. I'm told the truth, in part, is that a lot of the time this would be to restrain her from trying to hit him with a poker or whatever she had picked up because he had come home drunk again; she had quite a temper! Whatever the reason, my dad grew up in and around conflict and violence.

Nana finally left him when my dad was in his mid-teens,

which was a monumental decision on her part because in those days, separation in marriage was frowned upon by society, whatever the reasons behind it, but by then the damage was done. Despite wanting for nothing materially, which contributed to him being lazy and lacking a good work ethic, he had also been exposed to drunkenness, violence and aggression as a normal part of family life. He had become a product of his environment and negative life experiences whilst growing up, and seemed unable to break the generational cycle.

It is no wonder then that dad began to display similar destructive habits in the early years of his family life. As I mentioned earlier, he became abusive and violent towards mum even before I was born; a behaviour that continued to shape our family life and became a major cause of pain in the lives of many people, especially to those closest to him.

I guess mum must have loved him, or maybe she lived in fear of him. She certainly lived in hope that he would change. but he didn't, and the violence and abuse would continue for the next fifteen years.

Just in case you are wondering if my mum was some weak and timid person for putting up with that treatment, let me correct you; that is far from the truth. She was about five feet four inches tall with piercing blue eyes and fiery red hair. Back in the day, she was as tough as they came! I've seen her stand toe-to-toe with both men and women far bigger than her – some of those tales will tumble out as our story unfolds.

So there we were, becoming a repeat of our parent's generation, while surviving on benefits, milk tokens and free school dinners – in fact, anything that was free! Not that I noticed when I was very young, an environment of poverty was just my 'norm'. It was only as I started getting a little older that I began to notice the differences between me and my other friends, particularly at school.

School

I vividly remember my first day at school. The reception class had its own separate classroom and play area at the rear of the victorian redbrick school, presumably to help the new children integrate into school life without being overwhelmed by the boisterous older kids. It was a 1950's built, prefabricated unit with its own little play area separate from the main school playground.

The main school seemed to stand proudly; overshadowing our little classroom. It had steeply pitched rooves, ornate window openings and feature brick details at the corners and on the gutter line. Inside, its ceilings were vaulted which made every single noise echo and reverberate around the building.

I found that first day frightening. The noise of all the children and the sheer scale of the place frightened the life out of me and I clung to mum for dear life. She took me into my class and stayed with me for a little while to help me get used to my surroundings. But then she finally told me she was going and she left. I was horrified. I ran to the window and began shouting for her. Whether she could hear me or not, I don't know, but she just kept on walking without ever glancing back. I cried my eyes out. I can still picture it now, me standing by a floor to ceiling window, crying and pleading with her to come back for me. A teacher tried to comfort me, but I was having none of it and wriggled free from her comforting arm to continue my tearful pleading by the window. Of course, it didn't work and she didn't come back until home time, by which time I'd settled down and eventually actually enjoyed my first day at school. It's amazing how powerful our memories can be from those formative moments of life.

The school was called Ledger Lane Infants and mrs Lunn was the Headmistress. All I can remember of her is that she was a petite woman who walked around with her shoulders back, oozing an air of stern authority. Her hair was pulled back into a bun and she dressed immaculately. She could certainly put fear and trembling into you when she told you off.

As you'd expect, my memories of those early school years are quite vague but one thing I will never forget was an incident that we as a family still laugh and joke about today. I would have been seven at the time.

It had been a normal school day and, at its close, we were being led in time-honoured fashion to the front entrance gates to be reunited with our waiting parents. As we got near the gates, I suddenly became aware of shouts and screams coming from somewhere in front of me. There was something going on in the waiting crowd but a wall of adults kept me from seeing what it was. Then suddenly, a gap appeared in the human barrier and all I saw was my mum fighting. All hell was breaking loose. She had hold of another woman's hair with one hand and was punching her in the face ferociously with her other. It was chaos! And all in the school playground! Mum kicked and punched the woman whilst screaming obscenities her. Some other mum's were wading in to try and split them up, whilst others were grabbing their children and ushering them away to safety. Some of my mum's supporters were egging her on – there's loyalty of a weird kind on estates like the one we lived on – and the teachers were trying to shepherd us kids back inside away from the carnage. It was madness, a full on fight in an infant school playground. It's no wonder I grew up the way I did!

It ended as the warring factions were separated, but not before mum had left the other woman on the playground floor, bleeding and bruised. And before I knew it, we were walking home. I looked up to mum with a new sense of admiration after that, particularly when I learned that the fight was over something the other woman had said about one of us kids.

Not long after that I moved up to the junior school next door and I have many fond memories of my time there. But looking back, it was also the time when the flaws in my character began to manifest themselves more obviously. Slowly, but surely, the generational cycle began to repeat itself again.

The cracks appear

It's now easy to look back and identify that the source of my social decline at school was directly related to my home life. So, let me give you a glimpse into the reality of it.

As I have explained, money was tight. Dad did eventually get the odd job here and there; always cash-in-hand of course, so as to never mess with his benefits. His only job of satisfaction, so to speak, was as a bouncer at a notorious club on the outskirts of Wakefield called 'The Roundhouse'. It suited him - he was paid cash, could drink all he wanted and got to smash people up who got out of hand. He wasn't the biggest of blokes, being about five foot ten, but he had an incredibly fast and hard punch for a man his size. And he was fearless. The guys he bounced with were older and bigger than him and had been in the game for many years, so he was the 'young blood' with lots to prove and he never disappointed. The morning after a shift we would often notice he had fresh bruises or stitches where he had been glassed in a fight the night before.

He was good at his job and loved every minute of it, but he also brought his work home with him and ruled the house with a rod, or fist, - of iron. When we were very young, we never saw him hitting mum but we could hear the commotion from our bedroom upstairs, and then we'd see her the next day with bruises and cuts. She tried to hide it from us but it must have been tough for her to raise four young kids while living with a drunken wife beater and in total poverty.

Then he began to start hitting us kids; mainly my older brother, Johnny and me. Back in those days most kids got a slap from their parents if they did anything wrong but my beatings went way beyond that. Whenever I did anything wrong he would just lash out and hit me with such venom it was frightening as well as painful. He would just explode with such anger and aggression, that he would hit me with the first thing he could get his hands on. Over the years he has hit me with cups, ashtrays, belts and sticks. He once picked up a pool cue and hit me with it, but he swung it so hard it snapped across my back and left me writhing in pain. Mum did try to step in at times but she would then get it from him too. He would punch me full on and leave me sobbing in bed for hours afterwards; terrified he would come back and carry on the violence. I don't know why, but I was the one who seemed to get the most beatings from him. I was terrified of him and yet loved him at the same time.

Please don't let this give you the perception that my dad was a truly evil person; he wasn't and there were times when he was a fun dad to have around. To me, he was the best dad in the world, because I didn't know any different. Those occasions were rare, but they were there, which demonstrated he was a man capable of showing love and affection, but it had somehow become suppressed and overtaken by the tyranny of violence and aggression.

Meanwhile, school life continued. For the most part I enjoyed going and was pretty good at my studies but my bad behaviour always seemed to get the better of me. I wasn't 'gobby' or disruptive but I always had a knack of being where I shouldn't be or putting things in my pocket that weren't mine.

The first time I got caught stealing was at the age of nine. I had sneaked into my classroom over playtime when we weren't allowed in and started snooping around the teacher's desk, opening one drawer then the other until I saw what I was looking for: money. It was only fifty pence, which is probably worth a fiver in today's money, but when I saw it I took it, closed the drawer and hid it in my bag – the perfect crime. The theft was soon noticed and a bag-search followed which resulted in me being marched to the Head's Office for punishment - a dozen whacks on the backside. I promised myself I'd never do it again, but that was a promise soon broken.

I also took another knock at home during those formative years, which just compounded my confusion and pain - I was sexually abused for the first time. Two girls used to babysit for us when mum and dad went out. They would make me undress in front of them and stand there naked before making me lie under a cover on the couch with them one at a time and 'do things' a child of my age should never do. I daren't tell a soul for fear of what might happen. But I was so embarrassed. It had the effect of making me very self-conscious and opened my mind up to things that I was far too young for.

And so a combination of poverty, dysfunctional parenting and an over exposure to the dark side of life began to shape my development. So much so, they became a merged normal for me. I don't think I truly realised how poor we were until I was quite a bit older, but I do know that growing up in poverty is a horrible experience to live through. A hand-to-mouth existence breeds fear and insecurities in people and causes them to do things they wouldn't normally do, simply to survive. The law becomes irrelevant and survival becomes paramount. I now look back and realise that our lives frequently revolved around breaking the law and hoping we wouldn't get caught, or simply going without. These shape a young life, and not for the better.

Dad was certainly never one to shy away from breaking the law. He used to take me and Johnny scrapping, which involved collecting discarded metal we could get cash for. The thing was, he didn't care where the metal came from. If he saw a bit of metal in someone's garden and no one was around, he would send the two of us in to pick up the 'discarded metal'. He reasoned that if we got caught – which we never did – we could plead innocence due to our young age, whereas he may get reported. He was like a modern day Fagin! We would also go nicking coal from the local colliery to use on our open fires. We just did what we needed to do to survive. We also discovered that carol singing from house to house around Christmas time was always a good little earner!

Calm in the chaos

Christmas is probably the time I remember most fondly from those years. It was a time of happiness and tranquillity in the otherwise chaotic and dysfunctional life we lived. Whatever mum and dad needed to do to make it a great time, they did. We always had a pile of presents to open on Christmas morning; and where they came from was irrelevant. They may have been 'hand me downs or from a market stall, a jumble sale or from the 'back of a lorry'; we didn't care and certainly made the most of it.

Like all families, we had our routine. The tree went up twelve days before Christmas and the house would be decorated. On Christmas Eve the booze and our soft drinks would be lined up along the wall by the tree. Even dad would be in a good mood. After tea, mum usually prepared some of the vegetables for Christmas dinner, and then she would let us older ones have a glass of Advocat mixed with lemonade – better known as a Snowball these days – while we watched TV as a family. We felt like grown-ups with a glass of booze in our hands! Then dad would let us have a glass of 'black beer'. I still don't know what that stuff was, even today, and it tasted revolting – but not as bad as the watered down sterilised milk! It was more booze, and for an eight or nine year old, that was enough. We didn't know if it had alcohol in it or not but the word 'beer' meant it was 'mans stuff'. Then it would be off to bed around nine, after leaving a couple of mince pies and a small glass of sherry out for Santa to keep him fed and warm when he came by.

We would try and keep awake as long as we could, talking about what we hoped we would be getting from Santa and claiming we could hear him on the roof top, until one by one the three of us would fall asleep.

Next morning we would bounce into mum and dad's bedroom, excitedly asking them to get up. But the rule was we could not go downstairs until six o'clock. Not a minute earlier. Mum would send Johnny downstairs to make her a coffee but he wasn't allowed to go in the living room – its door made a loud click when it was opened, so there was no way he could sneak inside without mum hearing it. The coffee would be brought back upstairs to mum and she would sit in bed and drink it, waking up, or sobering up, while we egged her on to drink it quicker. Then she'd come down with us and let us into the room.

The tree lights would have been left on and our presents would be laid out in separate piles, some on the sofa and some on the floor. It was always a beautiful sight, for at least two seconds before we began tearing at the wrapping paper around our presents! Paper would be flying everywhere, as shouts of happiness and 'thanks mum' would ring out. Then we would argue over a present that had slipped into the 'no man's land' between two piles and was being fought over by two of us until mum stepped in and gave it to the rightful owner. It was so much fun.

Then we'd play with our stuff and each other's stuff – more arguments – and start eating from our selection boxes. The chocolate always went first, then the chewy sweets and then finally the Spangles. Whatever happened to Spangles?

Dad would get up about seven or so and sit with us while mum went back to bed for a bit. He would sit with us and play with our toys with us. This was the side of dad that I loved; I enjoyed every minute of the time he spent with me on those Christmas mornings.

The floor was awash with every toy you would associate with those times: an Evel Knievel action figure with motorbike, Action Man with the moving eyes and rubber fist grip, Spirograph, Rebound, Mousetrap, Buckaroo, Rock-em sock-em Robots, Simon Says, Hot Wheels racing car set with the plastic track that curled over in a full circle, Meccano, Tonka trucks, Jaws – a game of fishing stuff out of a shark's mouth before it's jaws snapped shut. Star Wars figures, the Millennium Falcon, Thunderbirds (my favourite was the green Thunderbird 2 ship), Subbuteo … and the list went on.

The day would be one of playing, eating sweets and more sweets. The smell of slow cooking food wafted around the house and sounds of laughter would be everywhere, as well as the occasional argument between one of us brothers. Oh, if only life could be like this every day.

A massive dinner would be served around one o'clock and we'd all sit around the table with our paper Christmas hats on, fresh out of the crackers we had just pulled. After that, it would be toys and sweets all day long, or when a TV programme caught my attention I would put things down and plonk myself down on the sofa. The one film I loved to watch, which seemed to be on every year, was 'The Wizard of Oz'. We'd all end up sat around the room, watching the film, eating nuts and more sweets.

Then later on when dad was drunk, he would play hide

and seek with us, making us count whilst he hid, then he'd jump out of his hiding place and frighten the life out of us. These are the times I choose to remember my dad by. Just being with him and having his attention was precious. Having fun with him was all I ever wanted.

Back to 'normal'

Christmas soon passed, the New Year arrived and we slipped back into our normal routine. But beneath the surface things continued to deteriorate, especially for mum.

Sadly, the violence worsened. Managing it, as well as trying to raise us four boys, began to put too great a strain on mum so she went to the doctors and was prescribed Valium. And it worked to a point. It certainly chilled her out but it did the job too well at times. She lost her edge and we began to get away with creating havoc, which she would just shrug off or take no interest in. When the neighbours came round to complain about us kids, she would just tell them to 'F off'. She was on those tablets for years and although they helped her cope with the pressures of home life, they certainly didn't help our family relationships at all. Unfortunately, she was so far 'away with the fairies' that she pretty much ceased to have an empowering or positive influence on me. I increasingly became a law unto myself.

I had my first run in with the Police when I was about ten. One morning dad was fast asleep, still drunk from the night before, and I sneaked into the bedroom and stole some money out of his pocket and spent it on sweets at the shop. When I got home, dad was stood by the kitchen sink and gave me a look that put the fear of death into me.

"Have you taken any money out of my jeans?" he growled.

I just stood there and froze.

He lurched forward to try and grab me but mum got to me first and dragged me out of his way. "Have you got his money?" she asked me. I admitted that I had straightaway to her.

"Where is it?"

"I spent it."

"What on?"

"Sweets."

She told me to wait in the garden and went inside.

After a while, they called me into the house and as I walked in, I froze again. Not because of my dad but the local copper was stood in the kitchen with them both. So the story of my crime tumbled out in front of them all. The copper then gave me a lecture and told me I could be arrested and taken to the police station, which scared the life out of me. His lecture went on and on but I was distracted by my thoughts of what dad was going to do to me after he left. 'Crap! I'm in trouble now'. I almost wanted to go with the copper just to escape dad. To my surprise, after they had showed him out, dad didn't do anything, it was mum who gave me a good hiding and sent me to bed. Her good hidings hurt but they were nothing compared to dad's.

Unfortunately, the lesson I learnt from my first brush with the law didn't sink in and it wouldn't be too long before I would be seeing them again. Meanwhile, life continued on its rocky course for me and my siblings.

We loved playing out in the street, as I've mentioned before, and quite often we would be kicking a ball around between us. One day the ball did what it had done numerous times before, it went over into one of the gardens opposite our house. I opened the gate and went in to get our ball back when the bloke who lived there came rushing out, grabbed the ball before I could, and told me to get out.

"Can I have my ball back then?" I asked.

"No!" he said firmly. He was clearly tired of us kicking balls into his garden, so I can't blame him for his built up frustration, but not giving us our ball back was a mistake.

We went inside and told mum. She went straight over there to sort it out, while we all sat on the front wall waiting to get our ball back.

The couple who lived there were in their late forties and they had one grown up daughter. The father was still in the garden when he spotted mum walking over the street, so he rushed to the gate to lock it. She just stood in front of the gate and told him to give us the ball back. He then burst into a tirade of how tired he was of the ball coming into his garden and breaking his plants and so on. Then his wife appeared and added her opinion about our antics.

She must have said something that pushed one of mum's wrong buttons because without any warning, mum turned slightly sideways and launched a full punch into her face. Then, before the woman or her husband had time to respond, mum grabbed the woman's hair and started banging her head on the garden gate. Her husband tried to grab mum and started to grapple with her. So mum let go of the woman, who slumped to the floor behind the gate, and she started punching the living daylights out of the husband. He tried to duck out of the way but she was having none of it. She grabbed hold of his shirt, tried to bite him and then continued to rain punches at him.

We were all sat on the wall, fascinated by the spectacle and egging her on. Just then the woman stood up from behind the gate, her face covered in blood, with hair all over the place, crying and screaming at mum. It was now going to be two against one. Then from nowhere, dad appeared with a cricket bat in his hand, heading over the road to the join the fight. We were really excited now; dad was here.

The sight of dad approaching gave fresh strength to the guy to break free from mum's grip and he hurriedly rushed his wife up the path into the house. Dad did have one swing at him over the gate but missed. Obviously mum's tablets weren't working too well that day!

Then it all returned to normal. Except, we hadn't got our ball back. So I sneaked into the garden, got it and left without shutting the gate. Well, he was hardly going to come out again was he? Did they call the police? Not on your life. No one called the police on our family; everyone was too scared of us.

It had been just another life-shaping day in my childhood.

Self-awareness

One morning I was called into the Head's Office, which had become too regular an occurrence by this time. So off I went, wondering what I'd done wrong this time. To my surprise, I was told that I had been nominated as one of two children from our school to attend a 'talented young person' day at Bretton College in Wakefield. It was a new initiative to encourage smart kids in their learning, and give them a taste of further education after high school.

You see, my environment may have been damaging me, but I was essentially a smart kid with potential.

When the day arrived, mum accompanied me on the bus journey. No sooner had I arrived than I started to notice some things – I was at that very self-aware stage of a young person's development.

The first thing I noticed was that no one else had come on the bus. All the other kids had been dropped off by their parents, so I felt rather inferior. As the day progressed, I did well in the subjects we covered, but I became preoccupied with comparing myself with the other kids. They had nice clothes on whereas my shoes were scuffed and my trousers had a little hole in the knee. My coat had a tear in the back seam but theirs all looked so new and shiny. They seemed clean and well groomed for ten and eleven year olds, whereas I felt scruffy.

At the end of the day, as mum and I were walking down the long drive to the bus stop, all the other kids I had spent the day with drove past us in their nice family cars. I smiled and waved goodbye to them but inwardly I was cringing; I felt so embarrassed and self-conscious. More pain.

But it was soon dissipated by wider family news: mum was pregnant again! And this time it was going to be a girl, so she was thrilled. She had a tough pregnancy though and towards the end spent nearly two months in hospital due to complications. That meant we were all at home with dad.

Mum was worried about how he would cope but he was great. He used to send Johnny and me to the local supermarket with a shopping list to do the weekly shop, while he watched the younger two. We took an old set of pram wheels, with a big white clothes basket wedged between its bars, to put the shopping in. We would then push the load of food home while munching on chocolate bars that I had shoplifted from the store. Every weekend he would take us all down to nana's to get a good Sunday dinner inside us. He got away without having to take us to school, as this happened during the long school summer holidays, so at least he didn't have to get out of bed too early.

As a treat for helping him out with the domestic stuff, dad let Johnny and I go into Wakefield on the bus, to go swimming. How funny. I was ten and Johnny eleven at the time; these days I wouldn't let my kids out of my sight at that age, never mind let them go on the bus into town to go swimming!

We used to go to the Old Sun Lane Baths at the bottom of town and spend all afternoon there. I couldn't swim at the time so would stick to the shallow end. But one time I was showing off and jumped into the deep end. I just sank. I had no idea how to kick or get back to the surface so began panicking as I ran out of breath. I was drowning. Then an arm reached into the water and I was pulled out. I gasped and spluttered on the side until I calmed down. That was a close call. Back I went to the shallow end and stayed there, not really understanding how close a shave with death I'd actually had.

Mum eventually came home from hospital in late summer of 1980 with our new baby sister, Tammy. Now we were five little Haighs! Family life continued pretty much as normal except that Tammy's arrival meant that Jeremy had to move into our bedroom. So the four of us boys all shared a room, while she had her own.

Junior school was fast coming to an end and talk of moving up to the big school became part of our everyday conversation. What was it like? Was it true about how the older lads treated the new kids? Some of my friends became a bit fearful but not me, because I already had a big brother there who would look out for me.

3

The Ginger Afro Loses Control

I FELT like a million dollars the day I moved up to the local high school. Not only was it the start of an exciting new adventure for me, I was dressed for the part for the first time in my life. There I was, with my brand new uniform and school bag crammed full of the essential pens, pencils, protractor, rubbers, blank exercise books and my PE kit, all supplied free of charge because we lived on benefits. Dad had polished my new shoes until they gleamed; it was a good day.

On the first morning I met up with my friends from junior school and we walked the mile or so to school without any of our parents tagging along – another first! I felt so grown up. On arrival we were ushered into the assembly hall, sat down on the floor and given our class allocation. My name was eventually called out and I followed the teacher to our classroom with a lot of other kids who were to become my new classmates. I was in 1H.

Glancing around the class at all the new faces was a little intimidating to start with but things soon settled down as the teacher allocated desks to us in pairs. There were only two other lads from my old school in the class with me, so at least I wasn't on my own, but I was made to sit with another boy called Martin who'd come from another school. Fortunately, we hit it off straight away so my nerves soon disappeared and we got on with the first class.

Self-consciousness

"Have you seen the state of that scruffy git?" Martin piped up during our first lesson.

"Who?" I said, looking around.

"Him", he replied pointing at someone.

I looked over and recognised him from my visit to the YPO (Yorkshire Purchasing Organisation) where everyone on benefits got their free uniforms. As I looked a bit closer, he had on exactly the same uniform as me, except he didn't have a school bag. Instead, he had a white carrier bag with his stuff inside. He had written his name on the outside with a blue biro.

"He used to go to my old school", Martin said.

And then he went on to tell me all the reasons why he hated him, which were mainly because he was from a poor family and smelt terribly because of his poor hygiene. I felt very uncomfortable listening to all this, but just nodded in agreement and said nothing to defend the poor lad.

By the end of the day, it seemed a lot of other kids had reached a similar opinion about the boy and he became the subject of some nasty name-calling. It was something he must have been used to and, in fairness to him, he gave as good as he got, simply telling everyone to 'F off' very loudly, which attracted the attention of the form tutor who had stern words with all concerned.

Later that night, I kept thinking about my day and about how that lad had been mocked and ridiculed. My issue was that I had the same uniform as him – except for the bag. So

42

what did people think of me? What were they saying behind my back?

Feelings of acute self-consciousness flooded over me and I didn't want to go to school the next day. Mum asked me what was wrong but how could I tell her? So I made something up and off I went to join my mates at the end of the street. Over the next few weeks, the more this lad got teased and was ridiculed, the more I felt self-conscious. I now realise, it was at that point in my life that I really began to hate my impoverished background. I just longed to be like my mates, especially the ones with money.

My angst intensified just a short while later. I was walking through school to a class and overheard two girls making fun of my ginger hair. They had no idea I was just behind them. By that time my ginger Afro had a mind of its own; it was thick and wiry and stuck out wherever and whenever it wanted! Mum couldn't afford to send me to the hairdressers so she used to cut it herself with a pair of massive wallpaper cutting scissors. I'm sure you get the picture. Those girls certainly did and I was gutted. I just wanted to crawl into a ball and die. How I wished I could be someone else.

Another thing that didn't help my self-consciousness was having free school dinners. Each morning the poor kids had to collect a plastic token from the school office and then pay for our lunch with it. I was always a little embarrassed when I handed it over. Plus, the other associated problem was that no matter how hungry I was, the token only entitled me to one of each thing on the menu – one portion of meat, veg, spuds and pudding. But if you were paying by cash, you could get as many portions as you wanted. Well, I got a bit smart with this: I would walk along the counters and get extra portions put on my plate. Then, just before I got to the cashier I would take the extra sausage or whatever and slip them into my pocket, pay for the food on my plate with the token and then go sit down. Out of my pocket then came the stashed food, back onto my plate, and I got to eat as much as I wanted – including any bits of fluff from pocket!

So school life went on, I got my head down and studied well for the most part, whilst navigating the cliques that seemed to characterise most of my school years. There was the popular set of good looking lads and lasses, then the average set in the middle who typically turned out to be the most gifted intellectually and did well both at school and over the longer term, and then there was 'my set', those at the bottom of the pecking order.

I would love to have been one of the popular kids but I had neither the looks – what with my Afro – nor the economic status. So I just tried to get my head down and study as well as I could, while dreaming of being someone else. I do remember working out that it wasn't just the poor kids who got mocked, it was those who studied hard and kept out of trouble too; the 'swots', 'teachers pets' and 'squares' as they were called. And I fitted both categories, all of which fed my inferiority complex at an alarming rate.

As the weeks turned into months, school life took on a stability that I grew comfortable with. I found a group of friends who were lower down the pecking order like me and discovered I could have a lot of fun with them. They were from a similar social background to me, the only difference being that I liked to study and wanted to do well, whereas those guys couldn't give a rip. But I managed the situation as well as possible and our friendships blossomed.

Home front

In contrast to the relative stability I was finding at school, things at home were still far from stable. My little sister, Tammy, was growing fast and we four boys just about managed not to kill each other all bunked up in our shared bedroom. Mum was still on valium and dad spent a lot of his time drinking and staying in bed throughout the day. He did manage to get bits of work from time to time, always cash in hand, but the jobs never lasted very long.

Through my new school friends, I started hanging out in different places and one of our favourites was down an old disused railway line that led from our village to a neighbouring one. We called it 'the naggers'. It ran down to a couple of fields belonging to a local farm where we would hang out and make dens in the wooded areas. The fields were sown each year and when the crop was ready, we would help ourselves to a harvest. Johnny and I would bring home armfuls of carrots, potatoes, cabbage and anything else the farmer grew. Our favourite was rhubarb, which mum made into delicious puddings. What a luxury that was.

One time when we were down there stealing the farmer's crop, he must have seen us and the next thing we knew was that a Jeep pulled up at the side of the field and a big old man jumped out and started shouting at us. We ran off in the opposite direction, leaving our booty behind us and hid in a wooded area, planning to stay put until the coast was clear. Then suddenly, a vehicle screeched to a halt right next to the bushes we were hiding in. Now what? Should we stay hidden or make a run for it? Before I had chance to decide, I heard an almighty 'bang' and the leaves from the trees around me began to shake and fall to the ground.

"Run, he's got a gun", I heard Johnny shout.

And then Johnny jumped up out of the bush opposite me and legged it back towards the field. I wasn't going to hang around on my own, so I jumped up and began to run after him. 'Bang!' The gun went off again and this time I could hear the pellets flying past me and hitting the trees around me. I'd never run as fast in my life as I dodged between the trees and bushes, trying to keep up with Johnny. We didn't stop running until we were well clear of the field and half way back up 'the naggers'. Then we both collapsed in a heap, totally knackered.

When we got home mum asked,

"Where's the veg?"

"Oh, we couldn't get any today," we both said. And she left it that. Phew! We didn't go back for a week or so but we were soon back at it, only now we were a bit more careful.

Grounded

One of the lads I used to hang around with lived at the end of the street. Mark was his name. His family and mine got on really well together, so we saw a lot of each other. However, the problem became that me and Mark started getting into trouble when we were together.

I remember the first time it happened. We walked past a nice new Mercedes car and for whatever reason decided we wanted the badge off of the front of its bonnet. So we helped ourselves to it, twisting and pulling it until it snapped off. Job done. Then we walked around looking for others like it to add to our collection. This went on for a good couple of hours until a police car appeared out of nowhere, screeched up to the side of us and two 'coppers' jumped out.

"Empty your pockets out', they demanded. And out came all the badges. We were arrested and taken back to the police station.

The usual procedure followed. I was locked in a cell until mum got there, and then interviewed, finger printed and put back in the cell. Eventually I was cautioned for a first offence. I had, of course, been in trouble before but this was a whole new level. I was twelve years old and had my first police conviction.

Dad was livid when I got home and I got the beating of a lifetime. He set about me so viciously that mum had to step in and stop him before he put me in hospital. It was that bad. I was also grounded for six months – yes, six months. Each day after school I had to go straight to bed. At weekends I had to stay in my room all day and not come down. Mum would smuggle food to me on the days when dad would decide that I couldn't have any tea to beef up the punishment. This went on for four months, until mum persuaded him that I had been punished enough. So, as you can imagine, during that time I loved going to school, just because it got me out of my bedroom.

Sadly, my next arrest soon followed. Christmas had come and gone, leaving mum and dad skint and dad couldn't find any cash jobs. So I took it upon myself to get some money. Mark and I were out and about when we found a cast iron drain grate lying by the side of the road, the kind you find in most streets. So I decided to take it home as scrap, to get a bit of money. I left it in our front garden and then went out looking for some more. This was easy, I thought. They were easy to find and to rip up. So, myself and Mark were at it for hours until we had a great big pile of them in our front garden.

Unfortunately, we had been spotted and reported to the police, and the next thing we knew we were being caught in the act of pulling one up out of the road. Looking back on it, I can't believe how stupid we were; we were bound to get caught! So, off we both went to the police station again and the same procedure ensued. Another caution was issued, but this time with a severe warning attached to it.

The good news was that this time a miracle happened! Dad didn't beat me; he just said, "don't do it again". I reckon he felt responsible for being the one who had taught us to go 'scrapping' when we were younger. Whatever the reason, I didn't care. I didn't get a good hiding and that was all I was bothered about.

Gradually, my decline in life deepened. I started smoking when I was about thirteen and also began shoplifting booze to drink late at night with my mates in the park. Prior to this it had always been sweets and chocolate bars. But it was so easy. I would go up to the local shop and lift myself a half bottle of spirits, then I'd be off to the local park to meet my mates and we'd share out the booze. It was great way to spend my school nights. Inevitably though, my schoolwork began to suffer and I lost all interest in studying hard. I much preferred messing around with my buddies and paid little or no attention in class.

The one thing I did remain interested in at school was the rugby team. It had a good mix of the popular kids in it, which appealed to me too. We had a good team and frequently beat other schools in the district, which gave us serious bragging rights that I made the most of. I also joined a local amateur team that played at weekends, which was composed of virtually the same guys as were on the school team. We were very good, probably because we trained and played together every week both at school and at weekends. Rugby became my escape from both school and home life; I enjoyed the camaraderie of it all, the team spirit and belonging to something.

One weekend I didn't go straight home after a game, but hung around with my mates and went home later that evening. As I entered the house, I could sense something wasn't right. So I made my way upstairs, ran a bath and jumped in. As I got cleaned up, the bathroom door opened and in walked dad. "You're late and your tea has gone cold", he scowled at me through clenched teeth. And before I could say anything, he punched me in the face. My nose exploded and blood went everywhere. He just walked out.

I fell back in the bath in a daze with blood pouring down my face, which quickly discoloured the bath water. I couldn't stop it, I was covered in the stuff and the water turned deep red. "Mum, mum" I shouted, trying to stem the flow from my nose. In she ran and freaked out when she saw the state I was in. She instinctively knew what had happened and managed to stop the blood flow. He'd split the side of my nose open but a trip to A&E was out of the question. I didn't cry once; I was getting so used to the beatings by now that I was immune to them – except for the very bad ones.

Life goes on

The eighties were a great era to grow up in. It was the time of seven-inch vinyl records, Farah trousers, Kicker shoes and Levi jeans; ones you had to put on and then get in the bath to shrink fit them. Lacoste, Fila and Tachini were the must-have sports brands. Fluorescent pink and orange socks complimented our skinny bleached jeans – those were the days! Not that I ever had the money to buy them, I just shoplifted them.

Saturday was my favourite day of the week by far. It usually involved a bus ride into town where we spent the day fooling around with stink bombs from the joke shop before going to watch movies like 'Top Gun' or 'Rocky'. It used to make me laugh watching the crowd tumble out of the cinema after a Rocky film, all punching their mates as if they were Balboa! Then on a sunday night I would stay in and tape-record the top forty, always making sure I had a TDK 90 tape to fit it all on.

The rest of my free time was spent hanging around with my mates down 'the naggers' and over at an old disused pit, opposite my house – the one I used to nick coal from before it closed down. We would explore the derelict buildings around the pithead and then take turns to see who could throw the biggest rock down the old pit shaft that was still exposed and unprotected. We used to count how long it took for the rock to hit the bottom. I spent hours over there with my mates and a bunch of girls. After we had done all our larking around, we would each go off with one of the girls and fool around with them for a bit.

One day I went over to the pit to look for my mates but couldn't find them anywhere. 'Maybe they are down the naggers', I thought. So I set off back towards home and bumped into someone I wasn't expecting to see. He was an older family friend who used to come to the house and do a bit of work with dad from time to time. He was on his own too, so we walked on together for a bit and I thought nothing of it because I kind of knew him. But then the mood changed and he sexually abused me. There was no one there to help me. I was all alone and it was awful. Afterwards, I ran home and didn't tell anyone or speak about it until many years later. It became just another wound in my already damaged soul.

Life did indeed go on. And for much of the time I was still blissfully unaware how dysfunctional I was becoming. My self-esteem was deeply damaged and propped up by the random acts of violence, theft and vandalism that had become part of my so-called 'normal life'. School was no longer a positive place and home life was fragile at best. But things were about to go to another level and change the course of my life completely.

Turning point

One Saturday, I was hanging around in the park with my mates, when I heard my name being shouted. I looked around and it was coming from another bunch of lads in the park. They were from my school, but from the popular group. I walked over and was confronted by one of them.

"You fancy my bird?" he said.

"I don't know what you're talking about" I responded, and started to walk away.

Apparently, I had said something to his girlfriend at school the previous day, something I couldn't even remember. He ran around in front of me and confronted me again.

"Me and you, here and now," he said, and swung a punch at me that I wasn't expecting. Bang! He hit me full in the face.

I just stood there and looked at him. He wasn't expecting that. So he swung at me again and this time I was ready. I ducked away then hit him with one single punch and knocked him completely off his feet. I then jumped on his chest, my knees on either side of him, and started to punch and head-butt him in the face while he lay defenceless on the floor. I rained punches and head-butts down on him. I was in a total frenzy and couldn't stop.

After what seemed like ages, but which in reality must have only been seconds, I was pulled off of him by one of the older lads. As I stood, firmly restrained, I looked down at him on the floor. His face was bloodied and a small pool of blood lay by his head. Adrenaline was still pumping through my veins and my fists were still clenched as I struggled to regain my breath. All the years of frustration, pain and anger had suddenly poured out of me and this poor lad was on the receiving end of it.

"That's enough Tim, that's enough," pleaded the older lad, and he pushed me away so he could tend to his mate. As I walked away, I glanced back at him lying on the floor, motionless and covered in blood. Was I sorry for what had just happened? No way. I carried on walking, glancing back occasionally and was soon joined by the rest of my mates.

They had all seen what had just happened and they loved it. And so did I. I had found something else I was good at. But more than that, I had gained the admiration of my friends; I was a hero to them and that meant the world to me. As I walked home, I replayed the events that had just happened. I didn't realise that I had that in me. Wow, did I feel good! I told my dad about it as soon as I got in and was verbally applauded by him, which made me feel twice as good. I had the approval of my dad and my mates. Result!

Word soon spread about my exploits and I became the talk of the village. What a buzz! I loved it.

The following Monday morning as I was walking to my class, I was met by the lad who I'd had the fight with on Saturday. His face was a swollen mess and both eyes were black and puffed up.

"I'm going to f***ing do you," he said, and head-butted me without warning. I took it without flinching and immediately hit him with an uppercut, knocking him to the ground and I started to stamp all over his head and body as he lay on the floor trying to defend himself.

I'd erupted into a frenzy again, completely oblivious to the bunch of kids crowding around me. I stamped and kicked him at will until a teacher pushed through the crowd and pulled me off him and I was dragged off to the Head's Office. I got the cane over the hand for that little fight. But I also got something else I wasn't expecting, a new-found notoriety. I was the talk of the school because this lad was one of the supposed 'top lads'.

At break time, as I walked through the common room, I was called over to the couches where all the 'top lads' of our year sat. They wanted to know what had happened, so I told my story and they welcomed me with open arms; I was now one of them. What I soon learned was that in the murky world of gang rivalry that existed between schools, pre-arranged fights were being set up and I was destined to be on the front line. This was awesome! I had really made it, in my own mind.

The course of my school life turned around completely because of that one fight. I had a new respect in the school because I was good at fighting and I thrived on it. Some of the pre-arranged school fights came off and I was always at the front of them, nothing dramatic, just running gangs and a lot of flying fists, but enough to further elevate my position and standing at school.

One of the nastiest fights occurred during a rugby match against one of our local schools. The match wasn't five minutes old when a fight broke out on the pitch and that was the cue for everyone else to join in, including the lads on the touchline who were supposedly there to watch. We punched, head-butted, kicked and stamped their team up and down the pitch; flesh was flying as we laid into them with our studded boots. It looked like a battlefield with people laying around covered in blood, and it took a team of teachers to pull us all apart. After that, we became notorious among the schools In Wakefield and I was a part of it. I loved it.

I got the cane again, along with most of the rugby team for this little episode, but that was a small price to pay for the kudos we gained.

Things at home were deteriorating too. It was just after Christmas, for which I had received a brand new BMX bike. It was my pride and joy and I spent hours and hours out on it, whatever the weather. Then one day I came home from school and was told, "We've had to sell your bike".

"What?" I exclaimed.

"We needed the money", continued mum. But I wasn't listening anymore. I went into the room and there was dad, sat in his chair watching TV with four beers by his side.

'You've bought beers with my bike money', I thought. 'I could have shoplifted them for you, if I'd known you wanted them so badly,' I was furious.

What made it worse was that this wasn't the first time it had happened to me. In my earlier days, I used to go with mum to my grandad's every week to help clean his house and shop for him. He used to let me play with his model steam engines while mum did the chores. Happy memories. Then one day, news came to us that my granddad had committed suicide by shooting himself in the face with his shotgun. My brother had gone to the house and found him on the kitchen floor. In his will, he left his miniature steam engines to me. I cherished them and the memories of playing with them. But a few weeks after I received them, dad sold them without warning. More devastation.

I had simply had enough and that night I decided to run away from home. I left the house about seven that night and walked and walked without looking back. I ended up in Leeds and walked around all night, looking for somewhere to sleep. I had not really planned it very well and ended up very cold and tired. I continued to wander around in the cold of night until the police found me huddled up in a bus shelter at about three in the morning and took me home. Mum was frantic and tearful as she met me at the door. Dad was asleep in bed!

Sunday secret

I was going from bad to worse and then the strangest thing happened. Mum and dad announced that we were going to church the following Sunday. I never saw that one coming!

For some time they had been visiting a couple near where we lived called Paul and Ruth. Once a week they had a discussion where they talked about God and church stuff. Occasionally, us kids would go with them to this 'house group' and run riot while they were all trying to talk. Paul and Ruth were nice enough people and talking about this God stuff was OK to a point. But to be told we were going to church whether we liked it or not was not well received. I wasn't happy.

And so, as a family, we started to go to a little church in the next village. I had refused at first because I was too embarrassed to be going to church. But dad ordered me to attend, so that's what I did. It wasn't the kind of church I had pictured in my mind, with a steeple and gravestones everywhere outside, it was a modern looking building, full of happy-clappy people who always seemed to have a smiles on their faces. At one level I enjoyed going, mainly because I found out where the sweets were kept and I would help myself to as many as I could. I soon learned to say all the right things and actually enjoyed the bit of a sing-song they did.

But the truth was, I was embarrassed about going and didn't want my mates to find out. I would make up all kinds of excuses about why I could never meet them on a Sunday. We went to that church for well over a year but my bad behaviour carried on despite my secret Sunday activity. It was always more important for me to keep my new reputation up to retain my new found admirers.

Out of control

One day I was in a science class and one of the lads in front of me was mucking around and showing off. He was really annoying me. Eventually I'd had enough of his bravado, so when the class quietened down and he was getting on with his work, I walked around to the front of his desk and stood in front of him whilst he was looking down at the book he was writing in. With one sweeping upper cut, I smashed him full in the face and knocked him backwards off his chair and onto the floor. No drama or warning. I had decided what I was going to do and I did it in a very cold and calculated way. I simply walked back to my desk, sat down and carried on as if nothing had happened.

He jumped up from the floor screaming in pain, holding his face and trying to stop the flow of blood from his nose. The class erupted in chaos, whilst I just sat there. The teacher was shocked and tried to make sense of it all whilst tending to this lad. No one initially responded to the teacher's request for information. 'They daren't say anything,' I smuggly thought. Then a voice from the corner pointed the blame at me. I denied it, but the splash of blood on my shirt sleeve gave my guilt away and I was frogmarched out of the classroom and off to the Heads Office while he went off to see the nurse.

I was caned again, and suspended from school for a week. They escorted me from the premises and "don't come back until next Tuesday" were the last words I heard from the Head before he turned and walked back to his office. I didn't need telling twice and off I walked down to the park.

The perverse thing was that the suspension simply elevated my reputation further. So when I did go back to school my notoriety was legendary.

The truth is, I was getting out of control – behind my dad's back of course. My free time was spent hanging out in the park, fooling around with girls, getting drunk and vandalising stuff. We would spend our nights drinking, smoking, smashing up bus shelter windows and keeping ourselves amused with whatever else we found to do.

One night I bought some petrol and took it to the park with me along with some milk bottles. We made up some petrol bombs and started throwing them around. "Crash", they'd hit the floor and the petrol would explode into a fireball, lighting up the darkness of the night. We loved it. My friend Mark wanted to have a go. So he held one up and I lit it as he pulled his arm back to throw it, but he must have been holding the bottle at the wrong angle because petrol poured out of the bottle and burst into flames as it went down the back of his coat. His clothing burst into flames and he screamed out in terror. We immediately jumped on him and rolled him about on the grass, trying to put the flames out. Drama over, we got up laughing while Mark took his coat off to inspect it. Smoke was still coming from its charred remains; God only knows how he didn't burn to death.

I was always skint, which I hated so one day I came up with a plan to generate some quick cash. I shoplifted a book of raffle tickets and went around selling them, wearing my cub scouts green top and necktie. I'd left Scouts some time ago but still had the clothing and it made me look so sweet and innocent. The proceeds would be given to the local old people's home in the village, I told everyone. They sold out quickly so I had to go and lift another book of tickets just to keep up with demand. They sold out in no time too. Then I stole some boxes of chocolates to give out as the prizes and I went to the old folks home on the appointed day to hand over the money, minus a large commission for myself of course. I didn't realise but the local press were informed and I had my photo taken as the old folk drew out the winning tickets, cub scout uniform and all! I gave some of the cash to the old folks home, took the prizes to the winners and then off I went to spend my ill-gotten gains. Kerching!

On the move again

One day, mum sat us kids down and told us that dad was going to stay at his friends for a couple of weeks. 'Nice one,' I thought, 'they've split up'. She told us that they both needed a bit of space and time to think some stuff through but the reality was that she had finally had enough of him. And who could blame her? I was well chuffed. Dad left the house the following morning.

Everything in the house was great and mum was like a different person, spending time playing with us and making an effort to take an interest in us. It was great. Then after three days dad came back and the long and short of it was, he said "it is my house and I'm not going anywhere". So mum packed some stuff and left. Just like that, taking with her my youngest brother and sister.

I wasn't going to stick around with dad, so I followed her round to her mate's house and we all bunked up there for a few weeks until she could find somewhere else to live. Boy, it was cramped but at least we all got along while we waited for the council to come up with some new accommodation for us.

Dad came over a couple of times to try and talk mum round, but she was having none of it. She had suffered for too many years and now that she had finally made the break, she wasn't going back. I didn't go round to see dad again and I only saw my brothers at school or when we were playing out on the estate, which with hindsight was sad.

Not many days later mum told me we had a new house.

"Great, when are we moving in?" I asked.

"Tomorrow," she said.

'Wow, that was quick,' I thought. But then she told me where: the local women's refuge, or the 'battered wive's home' as it was commonly known in the village. I wasn't happy but mum said the hostel wasn't that bad and we would only be there for a couple of weeks, so I agreed to go. However, I soon regretted it.

It was a big old place set in its own grounds and basically consisted of lots of two roomed flats, each having a living space and a sleeping space. The bathroom was at the end of the corridor. I hated the place with a passion. The only remotely positive thing was that it was still in our village, so I wouldn't have to change schools or be separated from my mates.

The whole place had an eerie, institutional feel about it. There were no carpets, just a lino covering throughout the entire building. It was devoid of homeliness; there were no pictures on the walls, no nice colours or anything at all to give it the feel of a home. And it reeked of disinfectant, I mean it was so overpowering that the smell actually clung to your clothes so you couldn't even escape the smell when you left the building, it followed you. My mates at school could even smell it and gave me a bit of stick about it. But that was the banter that went with gang life so I put up with it despite my embarrassment.

A couple lived there permanently as wardens to look after the women and to call the police if trouble arose. The majority of the women living there had young children and, like us, had escaped from violent circumstances. It wasn't a pretty place. New residents would arrive during the night and I'd often see them the next morning with fresh bruises, looking shattered from their violent experiences.

The "couple of weeks" mum had said we would be there became over a year, but at least we were safe from dad; it was the lesser of two evils, I reasoned. I was fifteen at the time and had just started my last year at school.

Free from my dad's control, my behaviour continued to worsen, and mum increasingly let me get away with stuff, or turned a blind eye to things I was doing, just for an easy life. So I pretty much did what I wanted to do. I started burgling shops and outbuildings in people's gardens, I also shoplifted anything I wanted. So not having money became less of a problem.

Then one day I broke into a house when I knew the occupants were in bed. I snooped around in the dark and put my hand into a sideboard drawer. I wrapped my hand around something and pulled it out. It was a massive bundle of money. Bingo! I sneaked back out and ran off with my booty tightly clenched in my hand. Once I had got far enough away I stopped behind some shops and looked at the wedge of money in my hands. There was loads of it, over £1200. That would be four or five grand in today's money. I was rich now.

I spent the next few weeks spending it as I pleased, buying the best clothes and shoes that were in fashion. Then one day the police knocked on our door and arrested me. A fifteen year old walking around with lots of cash in his pocket had not gone unnoticed, so the police didn't have to do too much detective work to find the thief. It was off to the police station yet again, along with the boxes of new shoes and clothing that I had stashed under my bed for evidence. I hadn't hidden my crime very well, but I didn't care. If I wanted something, I would just take it without any thought for the consequences. This time I was charged with burglary of a dwelling and released on bail, but I went straight back to my old ways.

Tracey

One night, mum had gone out for a drink with her new 'fella' and I was on baby-sitting duty. Chris, the new fella, wasn't much older than me, maybe six or seven years, but he made mum happy, so I didn't care less about how old he was. She actually stayed with Chris for the next twenty years and I have to say this: I have the utmost respect and admiration for him. When he got together with mum, he also took us three kids on (the other two were still at dad's). He was the most consistent, reliable and faithful man a woman could want, and he helped mum get over the things of the past, paid off her debts and put up with my bad behaviour. I admire him greatly for the stability and reliability he brought into our world. You're a good man, Chris.

So, this night I was looking after the two younger kids. I'd put them down and was enjoying a beer that Chris had given me, when a friend of mine called round at the hostel. She brought more beers with her. Happy days. Tracey lived in the same village as me, was in the year below me at school and we'd been friends for most of our school lives. We sat there drinking the cheap booze and chatted like youngsters did, playing our vinyl records like you did until the kids were asleep.

Then we got it on together. I was well chuffed. I'd always fancied her but because we'd always been friends, I never thought it would happen.

A couple of months later someone at school told me, "Tracey is pregnant".

"So what," I said and thought no more of it. Until her best mate came up to me at break time and said, "Tracey is pregnant and you're the dad".

I was stunned for a moment and thought back to the night in question. 'Mmmm, that's possible' I thought to myself. But quickly retorted, 'no I'm not so do one and leave me alone". I walked off.

Then the rumours began. I was now the talk of the school for a different reason! My mates would call me "papa Timmy" and mocked me relentlessly. Tracey's friends continued to try and convince me that I was the dad but I was in complete denial. And I have to admit that I never once spoke to Tracey about it or offered her any support. I would see her about school, wearing a big jumper to try and cover up the bump, without too much success. I simply refused to acknowledge her or face up to my responsibilities. And so life went on, as did my destructive choices.

My day in court for the house burglary was approaching fast. When it eventually came, I had been warned there was a probability I would receive a custodial sentence because of the seriousness of the offence, so I went to court with my mum not knowing if I would be back in my own bed that night or in a cell. She tried to put on a brave face but I could tell she was hurting inside.

I stood before the judge and listened as the proceedings went on, trying my best at looking sorry for what I'd done. Once all the details had been aired, the time came for the sentencing. I was fined and put on probation due to my family circumstances. 'Well, at least I'd not been sent down'

I thought to myself. And as for the fine, how silly was that! We were broke in the first place, which is why I'd become a thief, and now I would have to steal more stuff to pay the fine.

The violence that had come to characterise my high school years also brought them to a close. It was one of the lads' birthdays and we decided to find him and give him the bumps plus a few extra digs of course. We found him at lunch time, grabbed him and started to hand out the bumps and a few punches to the arms and legs, when one of my mates hit him between the legs. As soon as we let go of him, he jumped up and lashed out at the lad who'd punched him in the 'family jewels' and punched him. A scuffle then broke out and I jumped in to stop it, but this lad swung at me. I ducked out of the way and waded straight into him, punching and kicking him to the ground.

What had started out as a bit of fun had gone horribly wrong and before I knew it, this lad was laid on the floor with blood pouring out from a two-inch gash on his forehead. Off I went to the Head's Office and was suspended again, this time for two weeks, which actually ended my school days. Because my exams were coming up, I was told to stay away and only come back to take my exams. Happy days, no more school.

I came back for my exams, for which I had done no preparation, and failed them all except Engineering Workshop for which I got a 'C'. Did I care? Not on your life. The main thing was that I was now free from school and had my whole life ahead of me.

It was the 23rd of July 1987. A few weeks earlier I'd left school and was now just sixteen. I didn't have a care in the world and hadn't given any serious thought to my future.

I was simply too busy, consumed by my own little world and enjoying the prospects of my new freedom.

That same day was, however, very different for a young girl of fifteen, who lay in a hospital bed about to give birth. She must have felt afraid and very scared, not just because of the impending pain of giving birth, but because she knew she couldn't keep her baby. The decision had already been made and she knew it. Only she knows the soul-destroying pain she felt that day. At 9:40pm on that summer evening, a beautiful boy was born into this world, weighing in at 8lb 3oz.

But Tracey couldn't hold him. She couldn't gaze lovingly into his eyes like other mums do; she couldn't check his fingers and toes or inhale that wonderful smell of new baby. He was immediately taken from her by a nurse and carried into an adjoining room, where he was checked by a doctor, dressed and placed in a crib.

"Click" went the camera and he was taken away.

The nurse returned to the delivery room and handed the photo to the young girl. Tracey looked at it and held it tight. She was alone with her thoughts, her pain and barely a memory of her beautiful boy. She called him Jon.

4

University of Crime

I WAS free, free from school and free to shape my future. It was intoxicating. The only problem was, I had no idea what to do next.

Some of my friends were going on to college and others were going into the school sixth form. Others had found jobs of various kinds. And me? I didn't know what I was doing next Wednesday never mind beyond that.

Just before school finished, I had approached the Head of Sixth Form to ask if I could come back to school and continue with my studies. He thought I was joking! But when he realised I was serious he politely told me, in no uncertain terms, that the school had fulfilled its legal obligation to educate me and that was that. In other words, not on your life!

All change

I was, of course, skint. A plan was needed, so my mate and I decided to set up a window cleaning business. Simple. Off we went knocking on doors around our village, asking if folks wanted their windows cleaning. Within three hours we had about forty names in our book. Now we needed equipment. So we got ourselves a set of pram wheels and

I nicked a pair of ladders from someone's back garden. Then we bought some leathers and sponges and off we went, pushing our newly acquired ladders around on the pram wheels.

At the end of our first day we had over £100 in cash. Happy days. 'This is easy,' I thought, as we headed off to the bookies to put on a couple of each way bets.

Each week, as we did our round, more people would stop us and ask us to do their windows too. So the round grew from one to two, then three days a week. We worked when we fancied it, picking and choosing how much or little we wanted to do. I ranked this as my second successful enterprise in life, the raffle tickets scheme having been the first. It was going well – very well – and it was legal! I spent that summer enjoying what I earned and was happy for the first time in a long time. I had cash in my pocket, a steady girlfriend, some great mates and a good pub to go drinking in. What more could I wish for?

That summer we also got the news that mum had been given a council house on an estate at the opposite side of town. My immediate thought was, 'Great, the sooner we are out of this place the better'. But then came the downer: it was in a place called Tingley, a council estate that was as rough as they come. And to make things worse, our house was smack bang in the middle of the estate on a street known as the 'tin houses'. They were post-war prefabricated houses built in the 1950's with an outer covering of tin; they were hideous and a total embarrassment for any self-respecting, cool guy like me to live in. On the up side, it was near to mum's family and I had no enemies there – not yet anyway.

Like most estates, it had a core of lads who guarded their

territory fiercely, so I always tried to get on and off the estate as quickly and quietly as I could, travelling by bus to meet my mates and see my girlfriend.

Life continued quite uneventfully until one night, as I was hanging out at the youth club, my girlfriend pulled me to one side.

"I'm pregnant!" she said.

"What?" I replied. I was stunned.

"And I have to have an abortion," she continued.

"I don't understand," I said, somewhat confused by this shock revelation. I mean, two minutes ago I was running around like any other sixteen year old, and now this!

She went on to tell me how things had gone at home when she told her parents and it wasn't good. They were successful business people and the bottom line was that they didn't really like me. I was not the kind of son-in-law they had envisaged for their princess daughter, so she had been told to have an abortion or leave the family home. It was that stark a choice. Wow, not quite the loving parents I'd imagined them to be.

I can't blame her for choosing the abortion. After all, who was I to offer her any kind of stability? I resented not being included in the conversation but then remembered the last time it happened, I had deliberately avoided getting involved in the decision. What a muddle my love life was.

"And I'm going to have to break off with you for a while," she continued.

"Why, what's that got to do with it?" I retorted, trying to be mature about it. But I was really angry.

"They are not letting me out until it's all done, that's why," she continued. "And I'm only out tonight so I could tell you in person," she trailed off.

I got it. "OK, you do what you have to do", I said. And that was that.

We parted and I sullenly made my way back home. I was gutted. Mum wanted to know what was wrong, in the way that only mums do. All she got out of me was "women!" and I went to my room.

Better news arrived a couple of days later. I'd applied for work at the local mill, on the edge of the housing estate, and I got it. So I reasoned that if I played my cards right and made a few selective friendships at work, I could get in with the lads on the estate and all would be well.

Work at the mill was exciting to start with and I got stuck into making friends as I went along. Thursday was payday and in my first small brown envelope I remember getting £126 and a few pence. I was buzzing! The new trainers I could buy at the weekend began to dominate my thoughts and then one of the local lads asked me if I fancied joining them at the pub that night. I quickly agreed; my day was just getting better and better.

We met at 7 o'clock sharp at the Bull's Head and I had a great night making friends and becoming a familiar face to the locals. I was settling in nicely. At one point, as I was putting a few quid in the 'one armed bandit', the machine began to flash its lights telling me I had some 'nudges' to use. While I was trying to figure out my best options, a lad who had been watching me swooped in without asking and began pressing buttons and nudging my reels. Before I had time to protest, he had lined the reels up and I won the jackpot! Four whole pounds.

'Good lad,' I thought, now engaging him with a smile.

"Alright?" he proffered, "I'm Clarky".

"Nice one", I said, "I'm Tim". And we ended up hanging

out at the pub all night. I got on so well with him that we've now been friends for nearly thirty years. But more of that later.

Another friend I made that night was one of the girls who worked at the mill. She came over and introduced herself and we hit it off straight away. So, I had a good night all round and my plans to 'fit in' were taking shape nicely. Roll on next Thursday! In the meantime, I spent the weekend with my mates down in Wakefield, flashing the remains of my cash and treating them to some booze – which I shoplifted. Just because I had money in my pocket didn't mean I had to spend it when I could steal instead.

Trouble ahead

Before I knew it, Thursday came around again. With a spring in my step I got ready, shoved some money in my pocket and headed off to the Bull's Head again. I was looking forward to another good night; little did I know that events would unfold rather differently.

I got there bang on 7 o'clock as the doors were opening, met Clarky and spent some time drinking and playing on the 'bandits'. We were having a good laugh, like you do, when the girl I had met last week caught my eye again. "I'm in there," I told Clarky and moved over to her table, leaving him with some of the other lads. We spent an hour or so, talking and laughing, with me trying to impress her with my best chat up lines.

A bit later I went to the toilets, where I was greeted by a voice that announced, "That's my girl you're with". I looked around and saw a lad standing just to one side, staring menacingly at me. "She's with me", he repeated.

Then without warning, he took a swing at me. In a split second I dodged out of the way of his fist and pushed him away.

"I don't want trouble with you", I said, quickly trying to make sense of what was happening. "If that's your girl I'm talking to, then I'll leave it out," I continued.

"Too late for that," he said and came at me again.

This time I was ready and as he pulled back his arm to punch me, I got in there first and punched him so hard he fell backwards and stumbled into the women's toilet door. I pounced on him, pushed him through the door and onto the floor of the toilets. The door closed behind us and he started to say something but I just erupted. A 'red mist' came over me and I started punching him as he lay on the floor. I just laid into him, anywhere where I could hurt him. Then, as he used his arms to protect himself from the blows, I stood over him and began kicking and stamping on him mercilessly. I was in a frenzy and blood was flying everywhere. It was all over the floor and splattered across the white wall tiles. I only stopped kicking him when I slipped in the blood and fell on him. I was exhausted.

His screams had alerted people in the pub and the biggest bloke I have ever seen in my life suddenly thrust the toilet door open. He was huge, with a big bald head and I had no intention of standing toe to toe with him. I was too knackered anyway. He tried to help his mate to his feet while I just stood there watching, amused that they both kept slipping on the blood on the floor – being rather drunk didn't help matters either. The first lad got himself over to the sinks and sat on the floor, with blood still pouring from cuts on his face, while the big guy told me in no uncertain terms what he was going to do to me. I was trapped and helpless, because he stood between me and the door. He began to take his coat off, so I knew what was coming my way. Then, as he stepped aside to put it on one of the sinks, I saw my chance and rushed past him like a flash to make my escape.

I hurried through the crowded pub to what I thought was freedom. But no sooner had I got outside than a gang of lads, who'd followed me out, confronted me. One of them came at me without warning and, just in time, I stepped out of the way and punched him to the ground. Then I laid into him with kicks and stamps while keeping one eye on the gathering crowd. Women were screaming, blokes were shouting and one of them was shouting at the lad on the floor saying, "If you don't get up and start fighting back I'll f***ing do you myself".

It was getting way out of hand and I was exhausted, so I just concentrated on keeping the lad from getting back up. I had to make him stay down, so every kick became an attempt to knock him out so that the fight would end. I couldn't go on much longer. Then, a bloke stepped forward, pushed me off the lad and said, "Go home! Get out of here!" And I was gone, without even looking back.

Exhausted, I tumbled into the house where I told mum and Chris what had happened. Chris had grown up in the area, so knew the lads I was talking about which was some comfort. I went upstairs to get cleaned up but the adrenaline was still pumping hard and I started to shake uncontrollably. Eventually it subsided and I went downstairs to get a beer and calm down.

'Well, at least I got out of there,' I thought to myself as I relaxed in the chair, replaying the events of that evening in my mind's eye. The moment of reflection was broken by a noise on the street outside. I went to investigate and before mum or Chris could stop me, I opened the door and recognised the lad who was making all the noise as one of the faces I had seen outside the pub. The second he spotted me, he came running towards the house shouting abuse, so I quickly shut the door, locked it and stepped back. An almighty crash followed as the lad lunged at the door with a flying kick that smashed it in. And there he lay in a heap on our hallway floor with his leg trapped by the smashed up door. What a mess! The next thing I knew, mum moved passed me and pulled a massive carving knife out from her dressing gown pocket and waved it threateningly at the lad in a heap in our hallway.

"You get the f*** out of my house," she screamed. "I have kids up them stairs and I'll stab you if you come any further into this house". The lad shuffled his way back into the garden, got to his feet and brushed himself off while still shouting about what he was going to do to me. Mum just stood in the doorway, among the remains of our front door, with the carving knife in her hand. She was so fired up that if he had made one single move, she would have plunged that thing straight into him.

He never made a move but continued to demand I go outside and fight him.

"You do know he's only sixteen?" mum screamed at him. "And unless you get out now, the cops are coming". On that, her final threat, he fell quiet and was gone in a flash. We found out later that he was on a suspended sentence for something, so if the police had come he would have been taken straight to jail.

Chris and I patched up the door as best we could and off we went to try and get some sleep. Believe it or not, my younger brother and sister never heard a thing and slept through it all!

On the following morning he turned up in a better frame of mind, paid mum for a new front door and apologised for what he'd done. It turned out Chris knew him from growing up in the area, so they made up their differences with no love lost. His mitigating plea was that he hadn't expected someone as young as me could kick two of his older mates up and down the pub like I'd done; all of which made me the talk of the estate. Being so young only added to my notoriety; I was now getting out of control and could just explode with little or no provocation.

Meanwhile, the gang fights back in Wakefield were hitting new levels of frequency and violence in what had become a kind of 'turf war'. Even though I lived miles away, I still went over most nights to hang out with the lads; after all, I needed to keep a low profile in Tingley after the pub fights.

One night we were out looking for the other gangs and we spotted one lad coming out of his girlfriend's house, which happened to be on our 'turf'. He saw us and ran off but we eventually cornered him in a bus stop. I set about him, watched by my gang mates; all he could do was curl up on the floor and try to survive the kicking he was getting. Punches, kicks and stamps aimed at his face and head rained down on him. When I'd finished with him, my mates took it in turns to do more damage until he lay there, a bloody mess. We walked off laughing and joking, and the last thing I saw as I glanced back, was him struggling to his feet and shuffling off down the street.

After that night, the atmosphere between the gangs went from bad to worse. We had hurt him badly, so his boys were out for revenge. One night they drove to our village looking for me. They had only one thing on their mind - revenge. After cruising around for a couple of hours without finding me, they set on a couple of random local lads who were not even part of the gang. They jumped out of their car and after giving the two unsuspecting lads a good hiding, one of them took out a knife and plunged it into the side of one of them on the floor. As he did so, he growled, "Tell Tim Haigh he's gonna get it next". And with that they jumped back in the car and got out of there fast.

I was fuming when news reached me the next day and we went out the very next night on the prowl. No one stabs one of our lads and thinks I'm going to go running scared, I kept telling my mates. I was in a bloodthirsty mood.

It was nearly 11 o'clock on a sunday night and, as we drove through the bottom part of town, we passed three lads stood outside a takeaway. "They will do", I ordered, and we drove on to park up the cars.

We took up positions to trap the unsuspecting lads and then I began running, so as to hit them hard and fast by complete surprise. It worked and I was onto the first lad before he even had time to move; I hit him so hard it knocked him clean out and he collapsed to the floor with a thud. His mates were shocked and confused by what was happening, and began backing away. So I went for one of them while my mates set about the other. He turned to run but I was too quick for him and caught him within about ten yards and pushed him into a roller shutter door. Bang! I began raining punches on him; one after the other, until I caught him square on the side of the chin and he suddenly went limp. Then I took hold of his head with both hands and began smashing his head into the metal shutter, time and time again, whilst screaming obscenities at him, all the time trying to hurt him more and more. The sight of blood on his face just made me wilder and I tried to smash his face in even more, it was brutal. It was as if all those years of being on the receiving end of beatings, and the pain it had caused me, had exploded from within me and this poor lad was on the receiving end of it all.

I was snapped back to reality by the shouts of the take away owner. Glancing around, I saw my mates still raining blows down on one lad and the other laying motionless on the floor. "The police are on their way," he yelled. Now he had our attention. The lads started running back towards the cars and I let go of my victim, who just fell to the ground unconscious. I began to jog after them and spotted that the lad I had attacked first was still laying on the floor, some twenty feet or so in front of me. In between us was a raised brick flowerbed, about a metre in height and a couple of metres long. So as I jogged towards him, I hopped up onto the flowerbed wall, jogged along its length and jumped off the end into the air, landing with both feet on his head. The noise it made was sickening! I almost fell as my feet slipped off the side of his head, but I recovered and soon caught up with the lads.

The mood in the car was one of excited bragging and bravado. But I just remained quiet, content with the revenge that we had handed out. The next night we met up at the youth club, where we used to hang out, to discover the news about what we had done had spread like wild fire. Everyone was talking about it, and oh how I loved the feeling of importance it gave me. But I didn't give a thought for the lads who had been hurt.

The following Friday at break time, I popped to the

newsagents to buy the local weekly newspaper, just to see if anything had been written about the incident. And I was greeted by the front page headline: 'Precinct ordeal of terror as trio of youths are violently attacked'. I was stunned. Front page news! OMG! I paid for the paper, went back to work and found a corner where I could read it discreetly. As I read the report, the reality of what we'd done began to dawn on me. And the description of me was pretty accurate. But did I care? Well, it was a bit too late for that now.

I couldn't wait to meet the lads that night and show them the paper. The day now seemed to drag but eventually I got finished, went home to change and took the bus to meet the lads. When I got there, everyone had a copy of the paper. We laughed and joked, re-enacting the night in question, oblivious of any consequences that might come our way. Before leaving, we warned everyone not to say a word and swore everyone to silence, but one girl had other ideas and a phone call was made to the police station the next morning.

The following Tuesday I was called into the office at work. The door was closed behind me and two CID 'coppers' arrested me. They first took me home and my room was searched while I stood watching. Items of clothing and shoes were taken away in bags and off I went to the station. After being left in the cell for what seemed an eternity, I was finally interviewed and the evidence put before me. There was positive witness identification, blood on my shoes and trousers, and I was unable to prove where I was on the night of the attack. I was done for. So I held up my hands and admitted it. I was then charged and after spending another day in the cells, was granted conditional bail by the local magistrate, which put me back on the streets with an ego bigger than a bus.

Meanwhile, family life also took a major turn. News came, like a bolt from the blue, that dad was in hospital because he'd had a stroke and it was serious. All the years of heavy drinking and smoking had finally taken their toll.

As I've explained, we didn't really see eye-to-eye but he was my dad; the only one I had. And I found myself very confused by the mix of emotions I now felt towards him. After about a week I plucked up the courage to visit him and was shocked by what I found. He was hooked up to machines, his face had drooped and he was unable to talk. I was devastated and genuinely felt sorry for him. But what was I supposed to do? How should I respond? I was confused. But that didn't stop me making a big decision anyway. I went home and dropped a bombshell on mum,"I'm off to live at dad's," I announced. Poor mum. She was so upset but knew she couldn't stop me. And off I went.

Dad spent the next eight weeks or so in hospital so my older brother had charge over us. But did I listen to him? No way. I just treated the house like a hotel. It was always full of my mates and girls who joined us for long parties that stirred up no end of trouble with the neighbours. It was mayhem. But I didn't care.

Going down

One night I was skint as usual, and none of the shops where I could shoplift stuff were open, so I broke into a garage and stole some tools. I discovered it was easy money when they quickly sold the next day. So I did it again, and again, and again. It went on for months and I became a one-man crime machine. I broke into cars, sheds, garages and houses, taking anything I could and selling it on the next day. 'This is the life,' I thought. I'd stay out in the pub until it closed, then set off with my balaclava and little tool set to burgle whatever I could find.

Dad had come out of hospital by this point but was very limited in his mobility. So I carried on with my crime spree, just a bit more discreetly so as not to upset his recovery. One of the burglaries I did was at a large posh house on the outskirts of the village. I broke in and managed to steal loads of high value items. 'I'm going to make a killing on this lot,' I happily told myself as I sneaked off into the darkness.

In reality I was spiralling out of control, yet loving it. I was never going to stop of my own free will; I was just sinking deeper and deeper into my self-inflicted mess.

Another night, my mate Andy and me were waiting by a bus stop in the village where we lived, looking for a lad from the other side of town who was supposedly seeing a girl from our 'turf'. We had heard that he got off at that particular stop and made his way up to her house. But that night he would be meeting more than just his girlfriend! Sure enough, he got off the bus and we emerged from the shadows to confront him. He was off in a flash but I soon caught up with him as he ran into a garden, where high hedges cornered him. So in panic he ran up to the front door of the house, opened it and tried to run inside. I grabbed him at that point and started to fight with him in the hallway of a complete stranger's house. Andy had caught up by this point and joined me as we tried to pull him out of the house into the garden. The mortified house owner couldn't believe his eyes: two complete strangers were punching and kicking another complete stranger in his house! Pictures were flying off the wall and a little table went crashing over. We finally got him into the garden and kicked the life out of him while the couple stood in their doorway screaming at us to stop. We just jogged away laughing, leaving him in a mess on their front lawn. It was just another normal night in my downward spiral. I was past caring and couldn't give a rip about anyone or anything, until the police knocked on my dad's door and everything changed.

It was three days before my seventeenth birthday. I was in our back yard cleaning up some stuff I'd stolen over the few previous nights, getting it ready to sell, when I felt an arm grab me from behind. Before I could move, a pair of cuffs were snapped around my wrists. And off I went to the police station again accompanied by the bags of evidence that I had been sorting out in the garden. Caught 'bang to rights' is the expression!

There I was sitting in the cells again. And I expected the same scenario to unfold as before: interview, finger prints, being charged, then home. But not this time. The police had traced some items from a house burglary to a second hand shop in Leeds and the owner had CCTV which had identified me. They also had all the stuff I'd been caught with in the back garden, which included a number of things from the big posh house I'd burgled a few nights before. To my horror, I was informed that the local magistrate's Judge lived at that house. I was done for.

As the interview progressed, the evidence against me for my more serious crimes became overwhelming. And it began to dawn on me that I was no longer being treated as a petty criminal. The police were no longer considerate of how young I was, they were taking a very tough line with me. My solicitor did his best to help me understand the seriousness of the position I was in, given the charges that were against me, plus the ones I was already on bail for.

Let's just get this over with so I can go home, was my attitude to him.

Only to be told, "You may not be going back home".

Going to prison was now a real possibility. So I had to be as smart as I could in an effort to remove the possibility of getting into trouble at a later date for crimes I'd already committed. And the only way was to hold my hands up and admit to all the other petty burglaries I'd done too. Well, the ones I could remember that was. I got to 103 before being unable to remember any more. I asked for all those lesser offences to be bunched together as one charge and taken into account so they wouldn't come back to haunt me at a later date. My attitude was that if I'm going to jail for the big stuff, I may as well throw in the little stuff too so it could have no future hold over me.

The following morning, after trying to sleep on a hard wooden bench in a cold police cell, I was called up before the magistrate together with my co-accused. As we sat in the dock, my solicitor came over and whispered to me, 'The judge who is sitting on this case today is the person who lives in the house you burgled.' OMG! You couldn't make this stuff up. 'He'll probably want to have us hung, drawn and quartered,' I retorted with a smirk. My 'brief' just walked off.

So it transpired that because my offence was against a sitting magistrate, my case had to be transferred to another district so it could be dealt with in an unbiased way. 'As if that was going to happen,' I thought to myself. I reasoned that I'd committed a crime against 'one of their own', so wherever I was sent in the country, I was done for. So we were dutifully moved in a police van to another district and spent the next two days holed up in a cold, sterile police station awaiting our fate.

Remanded

Finally, we appeared before the court to appeal for bail but were unsuccessful. "I remand you both into custody. Take them down," was the last thing I heard of the proceedings. And that was that; I was on my way to prison, Armley in Leeds to be precise.

I was bundled into a prison van with seven other remand prisoners. Each of us was handcuffed to someone else in pairs and four police officers accompanied us. It was a rather quiet journey; no doubt because we were all reflecting on the position we found ourselves in. I found my thoughts drifting back to the days and weeks before: the good times I'd had with my mates, and in contrast the night a few months earlier, when my ex-girlfriend's mate had pulled me to one side and told me that the abortion had gone well. She was OK and back at home resting now. Just the memory made me feel gutted; how on earth could an abortion go well? But then, I had no one to blame but myself. What if things had been different? What if I hadn't been a troublemaker? What if I'd been a normal kid who could have offered her a better future? What if … ? So many questions. But then my thoughts were interrupted by the sharp braking of the van and the sight before me: the prison gates. Stark fear hit me as I took it all in.

Armley is an old Victorian prison, built in the mid 1800s. It has a large, foreboding, castle-like entrance gate set in a high stone wall that extends out of sight in each direction. The prison wing roofs tower over the top of the boundary wall and the bars over the tiny cell windows could be plainly seen. The whole place had an overwhelming sense of darkness and dread all over it, and it was about to become my new home.

The prison was an adult remand or transit jail that held prisoners whose bail had been refused – like me – and those who had recently been sentenced to a jail term and were awaiting transfer to their long-term prison location. Every kind of criminal imaginable was there. Some had committed crimes of a serious sexual nature, paedophiles or 'nonces' as they were called by the other convicts. I found myself surrounded by some of society's most deranged criminals: murderers, rapists, sex offenders, thieves, robbers and very violent men, all housed together with a handful of prison 'screws' to try and keep order. It also housed young prisoners like me, under the age of twenty one. In fact, the minimum legal age a person had to be, to be held at Armley, was seventeen. And that day was my seventeenth birthday. I had every right to be afraid, very afraid.

The tall, arched wooden doors opened and the van crept slowly forward into a holding area. The doors closed behind it while a team of 'screws' inspected the van from the outside, looking underneath with mirrors as dogs sniffed around the vehicle. A second large iron gate then opened and the van moved slowly into the reception yard. The van doors were unlocked and we were ushered out, still handcuffed to each other while we stood around waiting for our next instructions. I looked around at my new surroundings and all I saw were high walls topped with razor wire and it struck me that every window had thick iron bars over them.

"Move!" barked one of the 'screws' and we trooped into a large cell area that was already full of people. Our handcuffs were removed and we were told to wait until our names were called out. My mate and I found a corner where we sat down and chatted nervously whilst looking around the room. It was a strange mix of people: homeless or scruffy looking people, the odd well dressed one, loud mouthed lads bragging about anything and everything, and others just sitting quietly. The 'nonces' were sat in another section just across a hallway, for their own protection, but they could be clearly seen and all that separated us from them was a 'screw' sat at a table.

We watched for what seemed like hours, as names were called and the prisoners concerned disappeared out of sight. My turn eventually came. I jumped up and followed the 'screw' into another room where I was ordered to stand on a yellow line on the floor. A doctor said to me, "Drop your trousers". I just looked at him. "Take down your trousers and pants", commanded the 'screw' I had just followed. So I did and just stood there, feeling both embarrassed and fearful at the same time. The doctor took a very close and quick look at my 'manhood' and then told me to get dressed. As we left I asked the 'screw' what that had been for? "Just to make sure you're a bloke," he said impatiently. "Now stand on that line." Yellow again. My police file was taken from the top of a pile and my details checked. I was photographed, finger printed and told to strip again; butt-naked in front of three other 'screws', this was degrading now.

I was given a box to put my clothes in, and there I stood, naked as the day I was born, trying my best to cover myself. I felt humiliated. I was told to squat, checked for drugs and then given a new set of clothes to wear. I've never got dressed so quickly in my life. My very own prison uniform consisted of blue jeans (not Levi's) and a striped blue shirt (not Stone Island), a pair of ill-fitting black shoes and a man-made fibre 'woolly jumper'. Hardly Mr Handsome! Then I was given my prison number: DB3998 and escorted to another room where I was given a sandwich and a cup of lukewarm tea. They both tasted like s**t but I was famished so I scoffed them down and sat around again until my mate joined me.

It was a horrible feeling sitting there; I was surrounded by people but had never felt so alone in my entire life. The noise was constant; doors banged, keys jangled, 'screws' shouted, and the place stank of disinfectant, sweat and God only knows what else. The air was thick with it; incessant noise and a stench that reminded me of the hostel. My mate and me kept ourselves to ourselves, and tried to make light of the situation. But in reality we were both scared and trying not to show it.

Another 'screw' came in and called out about ten names, mine was one of them. "Haigh" he shouted and handed me a white card as I responded. I took it and followed him with the other guys down an eerie corridor into another room where we were given a bed pack: a woolly green blanket, two sheets, a pillowcase and a towel.

"Can I have a shower cap please?" I asked sarcastically.

"F off" I was told by the lad behind the counter.

"Follow me" chimed the 'screw' and we marched up a corridor, bed packs in hand, with a growing awareness that the background noises we had been hearing were getting louder and louder. He led us through a big iron door that led onto one of the wings. The clamour was deafening; we were greeted by all kinds of shouts, wolf whistles and obscenities from the adult prisoners. The 'screw' quickly looked at the white card we each had been issued with and pointed us in the direction we should go. He tried to tell us but he struggled to be heard over the noise.

I headed off in the direction indicated, and then saw another 'screw' waving us towards him from behind a metal gate. I passed row after row of cells, some with open doors, others shut. As I walked past one, I noticed a bloke just inside his cell with his pants down around his thighs, shaking himself at me, trying to tell me what he was going to do to me. I looked away and walked on until I reached the 'screw' at the gate.

"You two stand over by that gate", he said to my mate and me, while he took the others towards a different gate. I just stood there, trying to take it all in. Before we knew it, he was back and let us through the gate, which banged shut behind us, and he walked off.

The cellblock stretched out in front of me, four stories of cells on each side, with a big iron staircase in the middle, reaching up to the top level. Just above my head was a wire safety net suspended from side to side, no doubt it was there to stop people being killed if they were thrown or chose to jump from the upper floors. Each row of cell doors stretched into the distance for a good sixty metres or so up to the end of the block. Everything seemed to be painted dark or light grey.

Another 'screw' appeared from out of an office, looked at my card and told me where to go, "up the stairs to the top floor, second from the far end on the right." That was it. No one asked if I was OK or explained anything to me. So up the stairs I went, not realising my mate was no longer with me. This wing was quiet, something of a relief from the noise of the one I'd just walked through, as all the cells on this wing had been locked down for the night. I was met by a 'screw' at the top of the stairs who looked at my card and escorted me along the walkway until he found the number on it: B4 26. That stood for B wing, landing 4, cell 26.

He opened the door and without a word, took the card from me, slid it into a holder on the wall outside the cell and firmly helped me inside. The door banged shut behind me and its lock was clicked into place.

My new home

The cell was dimly lit, about two and a half metres wide by four metres long. It had a small vaulted ceiling with a single light in the middle. On one side there was a metal bunk bed and on the other a metal single bed. Two lads, who barely looked at me, sat on the lower beds. I guess they'd seen all this before.

I introduced myself and we exchanged some pleasantries. I was told the upper bunk bed was mine; so I climbed up, made up the bed and lay down to take in my surroundings. Not that there was much to take in; just a table and chair in the corner and a small arched window, high up on the wall, that had thick bars criss-crossing it. The silence was only broken by a little radio playing in the corner until the lads started asking me questions about who I was, where I was from and the obvious, what are you in for? Before long, I was busting for the toilet so I asked the lads about it. "Your bucket's in the corner" one of them told me.

'You must be joking,' I thought. But they weren't. I walked to the corner, picked up the empty white plastic bucket and stood there with my back to the lads trying to pee. I couldn't. Being stuck in a room with two complete strangers was affecting my plumbing. So I put the bucket down and climbed back onto my bed and just lay there letting my thoughts drift on.

What would mum and dad be thinking? What were my mates doing tonight? What would tomorrow hold? As my thoughts got deeper, I wondered about my ex and the abortion. Then for some reason I wondered about the baby that had been given away. I snapped back from that one, pulled up my covers and went to sleep.

My first day of prison routine began at seven when the cell door was opened. The first job was to carry my urinal bucket to the sluice room in the middle of the landing; it stank of stale urine. Then I collected some water in a jug to wash with back in the cell and tried to beat the toilet queue, but failed. The toilet door was about three feet high so everyone could see you sat on there and the whole experience just bunged up my plumbing again. Next, it was down to the bottom landing to collect breakfast, served up on a metal tray with plastic cutlery and a cup of tea in a plastic mug, which I then took back up to the cell to eat. There we stayed until 10:30 when we were let out for an hour of exercise, which consisted of walking round and round the prison yard. Then back to the cell until 12.00 when we were let out for lunch. Back down the stairs, pick up a metal tray with compartments and walk along the servery where food would be slopped into each of them by some guy, grab a pot of tea at the end and head back upstairs to eat it in the cell. We were banged up all afternoon before following the same routine at teatime, and then banged up all night until morning when it all began again. It was shit! That was my life, seven days a week for the next five months until I was sentenced.

The only break in the routine came whenever someone visited me or if I had to go back to court to have my remand status extended. Because of the nature of the prison, I didn't have the same cellmates for too long; they would change almost weekly or even daily in some cases. So I lived with a constantly changing stream of complete strangers in a little concrete bunker, never knowing what they were in for, except what they chose to tell you. It was scary. I was padded up with some right idiots over those months.

I never got into trouble while in there – well nothing worth writing about anyway – but plenty of it went on. Fights frequently broke out and stabbings, beatings and slashings were part of everyday prison life. But more disturbing were the suicides, especially given the young age of the lads on my wing.

The first time it happened scared the life out of me. I was woken up one night, by the sound of shouts and screams coming from the opposite landing. Some prisoners were banging on their door for the 'screws' to let them out screaming, "he's hung himself". Then the sound of boots running up the landing and the jingling of keys as the 'screws' raced to try and save the inmate's life. Shouts of "cut him down" and the sound of a call being made for an ambulance are just a few of the memories I have of it. The next morning, I saw the cell door taped up while the police investigated the death.

I soon learned that most lads who committed suicide would wait until their cell mates were asleep, then tie a ligature around the bars of the high cell windows, put it round their neck and then jump. There they hung until one of the sleeping lads woke up and found them. It happened five times while I was there, once a month. I got so used to it that the final time it happened, after the initial waking up, I simply turned over and went back to sleep.

Armley introduced me to drug taking too. I discovered that smoking some weed was a great way to pass the time but doing so fuelled a desire in me to try anything else that was on offer too. It became just another way of beating the boredom.

Over the months, I applied for bail to regain my liberty a number of times but was deemed to be too much of a risk and was remanded in custody, safely locked away from 'Joe Public'. This was before the introduction of the benefits many prisoners get today. There was no toilet in the cell, no TV, no game console, no duvet nor other niceties which I have seen when visiting prisoners in more recent times. In fact, the most luxurious thing I had was a small battery operated radio that helped to stave off the boredom. How I hated 'prison time' and its tedious routine; the only thing that changed were the faces passing through. Each day gave me more exposure to drugs, someone else getting a good beating, then throw in the suicides - it was horrible. The bathroom routine was one shower a week and peeing in a bucket unless a bored screw would let me out of the cell to use the toilet. Otherwise, it had to be done in front of your cellmates. And if I needed a crap, it was no different. You either used your bucket or crapped onto a bit of paper and threw it out of the cell window onto the yard below. We lived like caged animals.

Every now and again, family or friends came to visit me, which was an enjoyable break from the routine. But I think most of them wanted to see the prison more than see me. The only bonus was that their stories after visits enhanced my reputation and notoriety on the streets.

Five months in, my Crown Court date for sentencing was fast approaching. I couldn't wait, because I naively hoped that my time spent on remand plus my young age would sway the Judge to let me off with a community sentence. How wrong I was.

Convicted

I recounted the events of that fateful day at the start of this book, so you know the punishment I received for my crimes: three years of prison made up of a number of sentences served concurrently. Strange as it may seem, after the long list of sentences had been read out, I was quite relieved to learn they were all squashed together into just a three-year sentence.

So this was to be my life for the next few years. Bedtime came and after the cell light had been switched off at ten o'clock, I remember laying there in the quiet, still wide-awake and thinking hard. For the first time in a long time my thoughts turned to God; I even tried to talk to him – kind of, anyway. The weight of my mess weighed on me and I was genuinely sorry for what I had done – well some of it – so I asked God to help me make it through my prison time. I also asked him to help mum get through it too. I didn't even know if God was listening and I ran out of things to say very quickly. But it was a cry for help. "Please just help me" was the last thing I whispered before drifting off to sleep.

Next morning, in the exercise yard, I met up with my mates who had been jailed with me the previous afternoon. Five of the six of us involved in the fight that night had received jail terms but mine was the longest. They hadn't been remanded in custody like me so I tried to give them some advice on prison life but I knew that in reality, they would just have to learn the hard way, by trial and error.

Then the very next day, I got the news I had been waiting for: I would be leaving Armley in two days time and be moved to a young offenders prison near Hull. I remember thinking, "Thank God I will be out of this s**t hole before Christmas". I couldn't wait to see the back of that dump and promised myself I'd never step foot in it again. Something else I was wrong about.

I happily packed my stuff and joined a group of other prisoners making the same journey. It was quite a novelty, as I'd not seen much of the outside world for the past five months. Once again we were handcuffed in pairs for the duration of the journey and all the lads who'd been sentenced with me were on the same transfer. So at least we would all be together in the new jail.

After the two-hour journey we pulled through Everthorpe Prison gates and were escorted from the bus into a holding area. I scanned the place: it was still a prison in every sense, with high walls, cell blocks, barred windows and razor wire everywhere, but it looked clean and wasn't as domineering as the previous jail. There were even a few flowerbeds dotted around. Nice. After the same reception routine as before, I was allocated to my wing along with one of the other lads I knew, and we were taken by a much friendlier 'screw' to our new accommodation.

I was pleasantly surprised how colourful and bright the cellblock looked. It was only three stories high and half the length of my previous one, so not as oppressive as Armley. On the ground floor there was a full-size snooker table, along with a pool and table tennis table. 'This looks OK', I thought. I was allocated to a single cell on the first floor, which was quite nice considering I'd just spent five months living with complete strangers. I still had no toilet in the cell, just the white bucket, but I spent plenty of time out of the cell so it was for emergencies only. So, even though I was going to be there for the next few years, I reasoned it could have been worse, and was just so grateful to be out of that dump, Armley.

I settled in quickly and made friends easily. I already had one mate with me on my cellblock and there were a couple of other lads from my town in there too. So before long I had the routine sorted and got on with doing my time. The routine there was far more bearable. Everyone had to work a six hour day, then we got free time out of the cells every evening and at weekends when we could play pool and table tennis, do some weight training or just hang out. And I could shower every day if I wanted to. I was living the dream – the prison dream – after the nightmare of Armley.

My first job was in the metal workshop, which interested me because metalwork had been the only subject I had been remotely interested in at school. We made all kinds of stuff; some for charities to sell and make money, things for around the prison and things like hanging basket brackets and litter bins. I was enjoying it, until one day I'd heard that one of my mates was getting some stick from other lads on his wing and I came up with a great plan to help him out. I set about making him a nice big butterfly knife that he could use on the idiots giving him stick. I spent ages cutting the metal and the two ' butterfly' handles, riveted them together so it opened and closed nicely, and then started to sharpen the blade, when four 'screws' jumped on me. I was taken down to solitary, or 'the block' as we called it, and found myself up before the governors the next day.

I made up some story about why I was making it but wasn't believed. I got two weeks in solitary confinement for that little stunt. I then had to sign some paperwork to say that the knife could be taken from me and disposed of. I was later told that the knife ended up in the 'Black Museum' in London where people interested in crime and criminology go to look at related artefacts. Weird! But I guess it demonstrated what an unsupervised prisoner was capable of making.

After solitary I wasn't allowed back into the workshop – no surprise there – so I applied to work in the kitchen and cleaned the wing for a few weeks until a space came up. Working in the kitchen is the best job in prison because you get all the food you can eat and one of the best rates of pay. After washing the dishes for a month as all the new lads do, I was given the job of prison butcher, which I enjoyed and did for the next year. More sharp knives at my disposal. But this time I behaved and got my head down and served my time. Eventually I got bored and became the gym orderly and served out my sentence working there.

Drugs became another regular feature of my prison life, as I mentioned earlier. To this day people still ask me with some incredulity, "How did you get drugs on the inside?"

Well, we just did! I took cannabis, cocaine and LSD for the first time whilst in there. Drugs came in through visitors, were thrown over walls into the prison grounds and occasionally through a bent 'screw'. The 'screws' must have known what was going on and could surely smell it. But they turned a blind eye because it kept us lads subdued and made their job a lot easier.

The other thing you soon learn in prison, is the 'pecking order'. The 'top lads' run the wing and everyone else tries to find their place below them. From day one I made friends with the lads who ran things on my wing; and the knife incident only helped my reputation with them. We kept the other lads in line for the 'screws', moved drugs and contraband around and generally kept order. Two scouse lads were top of the pile on my wing until they were released, then I quickly moved up with another couple of lads and kept the place in order at the request of the 'screws'. I was well into my second year by then. My co-accused mates had been given early parole, whereas I'd been refused and had to serve my full sentence. I wasn't even allowed out to go to my own mum's wedding to Chris.

Soon to be free

As my release date drew closer, I started to take a bit of a back seat on things because I didn't want to get caught for anything and delay it. But I just couldn't keep out of trouble.

One night, the 'screws' asked me and another 'top lad' if we would have a quiet word with someone who had been making trouble for them. We understood. We would have a 'quiet word' with him, no problem. So that night the lad in question was let out of his cell to get something and we were let out too. As he returned to his cell, we followed him in and shut the door behind us. Before he could speak, I punched him and as he fell to the floor, my mate and me just laid into him. He began shouting and screaming for help, but that wasn't going to happen was it? He tried to hide under the bed but we dragged him out and as he jumped up to the window to shout for help, I grabbed hold of his head and smashed his face on the cell window bars. Blood immediately gushed out of a massive cut on his forehead but I didn't stop, I just kept on punching and kicking until he fell to the floor.

My mate pulled me off him and we had to ring his cell buzzer for the 'screws' to let us out because we'd locked ourselves in. When they saw the mess we'd made of him, they panicked a bit and locked him back in despite his pleas for help. Eventually another 'screw' saw him at his window shouting for help and came to investigate.

We were taken straight to solitary and the police were called to investigate the incident because of its seriousness. They questioned both of us and the two 'screws' who'd been on duty, but we denied it and stuck to our story. So in the end, after four days in the block, we were let back onto the wing due to lack of evidence. I got a quiet "thank you" from the 'screws' in question for keeping them out of it and was slipped a little something to enjoy the evening with. The lad who we'd 'had a quiet word with' was transferred out to another prison while we were in the block.

And then it arrived: release day. No one was there to meet me; I just slipped quietly out of the gate and headed to the station to catch a train home, armed only with a small bag of personal possessions, a few quid in my pocket and a mixed bag of memories.

I never gave a second thought to the fact that I'd managed to come through all that unscathed. But maybe God had listened to my prayer after all.

5

Hopeless Happiness

PRISON is supposed to rehabilitate guys like me, to prepare us for integration back into society and living life on the straight and narrow. But was I interested in changing my ways and building a better future for myself? Not on your life.

My attitude was that for every day society had kept me incarcerated, I was going to live it up and make up for lost time. But of course, I was now highly educated in the ways of crime, so had developed a range of new ideas about how to make quick money to allow me to enjoy my new found source of comfort: drugs.

On release, I decided to go back to living at mum's who still lived on the 'tin house' estate. I felt I owed it to her because she had spent the last few years visiting me in prison at every opportunity she had. Once home, I spent a whole ten minutes catching up with mum and the family, then headed off to one of the lads on the street to buy some 'comfort' – better known as cannabis by the uninitiated. Then I spent my first day of freedom totally stoned, while getting to know what had been happening while I'd been away.

I was surprised to hear that the world I'd known had changed. For a start, the rivalry and gang fights had almost stopped – but I'd have to see that before I believed it because I'd emerged from prison ready to step back into it, right where I'd left off; and I had a few dishes of revenge that I wanted to serve up to a few individuals. But apparently there was a new thing hitting the streets that had completely transformed the young adult culture. 'We will see', I cynically thought to myself.

That same evening, mum had arranged a bit of a family party for me at the local 'boozer' where I had a blast, getting drunk and catching up with everyone. They all wanted to know about prison life and I loved telling them the stories; it made me the centre of attention and I loved that.

Part of the way through the evening, one of my mates brought something to my attention that I hadn't realised: my hairline was receding! And what followed was a lot of good-humoured banter. But inside I was livid and embarrassed. The fact is, I hadn't noticed. Prison isn't full of nice shiny mirrors; all we had were small polished plastic ones that were are about as much use as the back of a spoon. Plus, for most of my prison life my chosen hairstyle had been that of a skinhead. So only now, as my famous ginger Afro started peeking out again, did I realise I was going bald – and I wasn't even twenty.

I was truly gutted! For years I'd hated my hair but now I hated losing it even more; it was a massive blow to my self-esteem and confidence. So to counteract it, I plunged myself into extreme bad behaviour. In a perverse kind of way I thought that if my behaviour became more outrageous, then no one would ever notice my inner feelings of inadequacy and self-doubt.

The world has changed

The next night, all the rumours I'd heard about a changed world were thrust in my face. My mates had arranged a lads party for me at a club in town; I couldn't wait! So I went and kitted myself out with some new clothes – after all my present ones were well behind the fashion curve – then made my way to the club. I breezed in and looked around, then froze. I couldn't believe what I saw. There were lads from other parts of town there, lads we'd spent years fighting against, sworn enemies! And my instinct was to go into fight mode. What's more, my mates were mixing with them. I was confused.

Ady, a mate from way back, came over and put his arm around my shoulder in greeting.

"What the F*** are those lot doing here?" I scowled, with fists clenched ready to go. He laughed and said "Things have changed. Let's get a beer and I'll tell you everything."

I was well confused but as we got the drinks in, I noticed that there wasn't a bad atmosphere; in fact, everyone seemed to be having a great laugh while a strange music boomed out loudly. We found a booth in the corner, a spot where I could be sure no one could come at me from behind, and then sat down and toasted my newfound freedom.

"So what the F*** is all this about?" I asked him, between glugs of lager.

"It's all changed," Ady said. "no one's fighting anymore."

"Why?" I asked, still confused.

"Because of this" he smirked, and slipped a couple of little paper packages across the table to me. I quickly swiped them up and told him to be careful or we'd all get arrested. I had no idea what was in them but I knew it wasn't legal. He laughed again and told me it was OK and just to be discreet as I opened them.

Now he had my attention. As I folded back the first package, I was greeted by the sight of white powder; quite a bit of it.

"Is it coke or speed?" I asked.

"Coke. Get some into you," he laughed.

I didn't need telling twice and I scooped up as much powder as I could get on my thumbnail, positioned it under my nose and snorted up the powder like my life depended on it. I emptied the remaining contents onto the back of my hand and lapped it up with my tongue.

"Welcome home," he said, raising his glass to me, stopping only to tell me to wipe the smudge of white powder from my nose.

"So, are you going to tell me what all this is about?" I insisted, pointing to all the 'enemy lads'.

He went on to tell me how Rave and House music had taken off whilst I was in prison and all the party drugs that went with the scene: speed, acid trips, magic mushrooms, ecstasy tablets and cocaine had turned all the gang members into drug fuelled ravers! Everyone was too busy enjoying their drugs and getting high to have time for fights; so much so, they were non-existent. Former enemies now sold drugs to each other and spent the nights getting high together and raving the night away. 'This is mental', I thought to myself. But Ady assured me it was true.

Yet it became a reality around me as the night wore on. People began coming over to me and welcoming me back, some were old friends and others were lads I used to hunt down. It was mad: I ended up talking and laughing with people I used to want to knock the living daylights out of and there we were joking about the fights we'd once had. It was surreal.

My powder then kicked in and I felt the rush of drugs taking over me. I 'came up' fast and the lads knew it and all laughed with me as I enjoyed my first cocaine high with them. The music was pumping and my body began to beat involuntarily to the rhythm. And before I knew it I was up on the dance floor, raving away with all my mates, new and old, under the energy of the drugs. What a night I had. The drugs gave me an overwhelming sense of comfort and joy; in an instant I realised how this powerful stimulant had transformed an entire young adult culture almost overnight.

I opened the second paper parcel I'd been given later that evening and found a small acid trip wrapped in cling film. At first I was going to save it for another night, but then the lads in the booth with me all pulled theirs out and we took them together. Drugs were everywhere and everyone seemed to have pockets full of them.

I loved being the centre of attention that night and the feeling the drugs gave me. I also loved the fact that the hatred and violence had gone, replaced by a newfound sense of togetherness and camaraderie that stretched beyond the boundaries of our geographical gang locations. This new rave culture was amazing and I was well and truly 'in'.

I finally got home some time during the following morning, not sure what I had been up or where I'd ended up. But one thing I knew, with the aid of drugs the pain of the past and all its troubles had become a distant memory. In its place I'd found a new sense of belonging that didn't have a violent side effect. Little did I realise that the side effects of the drug culture would be far more damaging and dangerous. But I was happy in my ignorance for now.

Money

I settled back in at mum's house quite quickly, leaving my prison mind-set well behind me. Her attention, as you'd expect, soon focused on the plans I had for the future with regard to work and so on. I didn't have any! I just wanted to make the most of my new freedom and enjoy the escape from reality the drugs gave me.

However, to keep mum off my back and my Probation Officer happy, I went on a bricklaying course at the local college. I actually enjoyed it. I soon met up with a couple of the lads there who loved to smoke dope, so we'd turn up early for college, sneak away and have our dope before spending the day bricklaying and building the models that were part of the curriculum. I was pretty good at it and being stoned helped me to keep my patience without getting frustrated. I was even asked to build some decorative brick panels around the college for visitors to look at. But I'd no intention of getting a full time job after I finished the course and came up with a perfect plan to prevent me from getting the jobs I'd applied for. I simply put on the job application form that I'd just got out of jail. Needless to say, the job offers didn't come flooding in! And I was happy with that. Plus I had a perfect excuse for mum and the Probation Officer as to why I had no job.

My only problem was that I needed more than my dole money provided to live on and sustain my drug taking. So, I reverted to old tricks: I went back out on the 'rob' again.

One of my closest friends was also quite partial to a bit of easy money so we started going out robbing together. We broke into houses, garages, cars, shops and factories, and took anything and everything we could sell and make easy money from. This was better than doing forty odd hours a week and losing a large slice in tax, I kept telling myself. The money I made was then spent on the weekend, partying and taking drugs. It allowed me to escape the mundane realities of life and lose myself in the temporary affects the drugs had on me; it was something to look forward to. Then after the weekend, I would be back on the 'rob' again to make enough money to enjoy the next one. And that was the cycle I lived for the next few years.

I should mention that I did manage to get a couple of jobs during my first year or so of leaving prison, just to keep my mum happy. But I hated them! I lasted two days at a biscuit factory and just under two weeks at a food packaging company. They helped me realise that factory life was not the one for me. And off I went back on the 'rob'.

Raving

The rave culture I'd immersed myself into was expanding rapidly in those days, and the race was on to hold bigger, better and more specialised raves all over the country. So we began travelling to more specialised events; to places like Quadrant Park in Liverpool, The Hacienda in Manchester and Shelly's in Stoke – all top venues in the early rave culture. For us, the travel became just as much a part of the night out as the event itself. My mates and me would meet up on Saturday lunchtime and all the talk would be about the night ahead; the DJ, the music and of course, what drugs we'd be taking. Then we would pile into cars or the back of a van and make our way to wherever we were going. The drug taking started en route, so by the time we got to the event, we were all high as kites and raring to rave the night away. Those were good days; the bond of friendship and camaraderie made me happy. I was just content to belong to something and be accepted for who I was.

One of my favourite Rave clubs became Hackett's in Blackpool, where at one point 'our crowd' and me went every Saturday for about six months solid. It was a two-hour journey each way but we loved every minute of it, filling the cars or old van with laughter, anticipation and lots of drugs along the way.

It was at one of the Blackpool clubs that I first tried ecstasy. Before then my 'drugs of choice' had been powders and trips, though I'd heard a lot about ecstasy as it was all over the news. The press made it out to be dangerous, so I stayed well away from it. I liked having fun but I certainly didn't want to die, so I kept to the so called 'safe drugs'.

One night, however, I was offered an ecstasy tablet, or 'pill' as we called them. I flatly refused. But the lad who had them was a good friend and he assured me I'd be safe and would really enjoy it.

"No chance", I said, followed with all the reasons why it would kill me.

"Well I've been taking them for months, and I'm fine."

Now he had my attention - he hadn't died.

He then went on to make a deal with me: he would snap one in half, take it and I could have the other half. I thought for a moment and concluded it was a reasonable offer and at least I wouldn't die on my own. So I watched him swallow his half and then nervously swallowed my half. I was past the point of no return now. The last thing I said to him as I wandered off was, "If I die, I'll come back and haunt you!"

Twenty minutes later, while chatting to someone, it kicked in. I was overcome with the most powerful and overwhelming feeling I had ever experienced in my life. Waves of euphoria and giddiness began to shake my whole being and a massive smile erupted across my face. This was amazing, this was ecstatic, this was like nothing I'd ever experienced before and I loved it! It gave me a feeling of 'love' that I'd never experienced before and I never wanted it to stop. I wanted to stay there, in that moment, forever.

The initial 'high' began to recede after a good hour or so and I wanted it again, desperately. So I danced off to find my mate again. I found him in a corner pulling funny faces because of the effects of his pill and I jumped on him shouting, "these are brilliant", trying to be heard over the volume of the music.

"Have you got any more? I asked". He just started laughing and, reaching in his pocket, handed me another of the small round tablets. After giving him some money, I simply threw it into my mouth, swallowed it and went off to dance again.

That was the beginning of my love affair with ecstasy pills. Doves, New Yorkers and Biscuits. They gave me a sense of peace and euphoria, something I'd been searching for all my life. They left me just wanting to 'love' on people and they wanted to do the same back. It seemed so perfect, so idyllic, and I never wanted it to end. But it always did because the clubs closed in the early hours of the morning and I had to make my way home while coming down from the drugs. When I eventually woke up the next day, I'd replay in my mind the events of the night before, recalling how the drugs had made me feel and the incredible emotions I'd experienced. But in that moment, I felt very low and empty. The high was good but the come down was far worse than anyone had explained to me.

This lifestyle went on for years: going to clubs around the country, taking life threatening amounts of drugs and dancing the night away until the clubs closed, when we'd tumble outside into the dark night, exhausted, wet with sweat and totally drugged up. Often times, because we were still completely off our heads, we didn't want to just go home. So we kept looking for somewhere else to go in the early hours; somewhere to take more drugs and continue our mindless binge. Sometimes we'd sit in the open all night cafes at motorway service stations or have our own 'mini raves' in one of the town car parks or in a quiet layby, until the police came and moved us on. A remote field would do, as long as we could park, turn up the music and dance around until the sun came up.

Other times we'd go to lap-dancing bars or seedy massage parlours and hang out in one of these for the night. We would always be popular with the 'working ladies' because we carried pills and coke with us; so we paid for their services with drugs.

I had descended into a life of drug-fuelled debauchery; a life characterised by dangerous liaisons and high stakes. My attitude was exactly the same as it had been when I led the gang fights: I had to be the most extreme member of the group. Back then it was extreme violence. Now it was extreme drug use. One pill, then two, a wrap of powder and another pill, never satisfied, always striving to retain my status as the 'drug monster' who never knew when to stop. Why? Simply to meet my deep need for affirmation and acceptance.

Spiralling down

My hunger for drugs became insatiable, especially for ecstasy, and I began going out to clubs on a Friday as well as on a Saturday. Then I began to include Thursday, just to extend my weekend. I'd leave mum's house on a Thursday evening and sometimes not return until some point on the Sunday, completely exhausted mentally and emotionally and suffering from my 'come down' after three days worth of pills, coke, dope and very little, if any, sleep. I then spent the next 24 hours in bed, sleeping off the residual effects of drugs before surfacing some time on Monday to get some food into me.

Reflecting back on those days, I now recognise that my deep desire to be loved, affirmed and accepted, drove the cycle of my life. Everything revolved around the weekend, when the drugs temporarily relieved my inner angst. Then when their effects wore off, and I returned to 'normality' my inner desires came back like a flood, reminding me that they needed permanent rather than temporary appeasement if I was ever going to be really happy. But I'd no idea how to find such relief, so threw myself into next weekend's oblivion with as much gusto as I could muster, just to mask the pain.

My spiral of decline became all-pervasive: it began to extend beyond the physical and circumstantial into my emotional and mental world. I became very moody and was extremely self-obsessed. I took no one's advice, not even my mum's. And my sole focus became the pursuit of inner fulfilment and peace through taking hard drugs. Sadly, it cost me more than I had ever wanted to pay and took me places I had never intended to go.

My drug habit and weekend lifestyle were essentially money-driven, and the amounts involved just kept on increasing. By this stage I was spending over three or four hundred pounds per weekend and robbing other people's stuff to fund it was getting harder and harder without being caught. So I turned to selling drugs to subsidise my lifestyle. At first it was small amounts, just to raise enough cash for the weekend. But it soon became such an easy way to earn money that I took to it to a full time level and stopped stealing. I used to buy in bulk, and then break it down into smaller amounts to sell on to my ever-growing customer base. Dope was mainly a weekday business and the harder stuff was for the weekend. I took bags of pills, and wraps of speed and coke, out to the clubs where I'd quickly sell out to people who were all too willing to hand over their hard earned cash in exchange for a chemically induced escape from reality.

So, the 'party' that was my life spiralled on downwards, like this, for over four years. Every weekend looked pretty much the same; a version of what I have described above, while my criminal behaviour reached new highs in order to fund it. And the easier the money was to get, the quicker I would be after it.

One time, a mate of mine told me where we could lay our hands on a safe full of cash. He used to work behind the bar in a private members' club that was out in the sticks, somewhere rural. It was a popular place, took good money and he knew exactly where the safe was – in a windowless room at the back of the building, so out of sight that the owner didn't think the room that held the safe needed alarming. So one night we went up there. In the early hours of the morning I spent an hour or so taking out the bricks of the wall with a hammer and chisel – my time at college was beginning to pay off! When I'd removed enough bricks, we climbed through the hole and emptied the room of all its stock, including the locked safe, which we moved with the aid of a sack cart. Once we got it back home, we cut the hinges off and laughed out loud when we saw the bundles of cash inside; thousands of pounds.

I stole anything I could lay my hands on to fund my lifestyle and never gave a second thought for the people I took from or the hurt it caused them. Quite frankly, I didn't care one jot; I was just consumed by my own needs. One theft that trumped them all was when me and a mate nicked a small yacht on a trailer and parked it on a bit of land outside his mum's bedroom window in the middle of the night. When she opened her bedroom curtains the next morning, she was shocked to see a yacht outside her house, seventy miles from the nearest sea. We laughed a lot about that one.

Another way I made easy money was acting as a hired thug. If someone wanted someone else beaten up for whatever reason, then I was happy to do it, for a suitable fee of course. I'd done it enough times in the past for nothing, so getting paid for it was a bonus. I just had to be selective about when and where I did it because of my criminal record. I knew that if I ever got caught for unprovoked violence again, I'd be looking at an even longer sentence, so I only took on this kind of 'work' if it was further away from where I lived.

The consequences of my lifestyle also began to bite. One night, the police caught me driving while high on ecstasy. I was banged up for the night until I came down from the drugs and could be interviewed in my right frame of mind. A driving ban followed and more probation for the offence of 'possession of class A pills and driving while under the influence of drink or drugs'.

Then, nearly a year later, I got caught twice in the space of a week driving under the influence of alcohol. So my driving ban was extended by another three years, I was fined and my probation order was extended yet again. I was lucky not to get a short jail term for that one.

I made a range of court appearances over those years for minor shoplifting charges and one for 'being carried in stolen vehicles'. Silly little things that I took in my stride, which in truth were all brought on by my reckless disregard for anything normal.

One night, while I was at a house party somewhere, I went outside in the early morning sunshine for a bit of fresh air and was greeted by a scene straight out of a cowboy film. In front of the house was a car with its door open. My friend was stood at the side of the car, both hands outstretched with a loaded gun in his hands, pointed in the direction of another car further up the street. Behind that car stood two lads who were both pointing guns back in the direction of my mate. Wow, it was a stand off. It was like I'd woken up in a 'Starsky and Hutch' scene. So what did I do? I went and sat on the garden wall to see how it would play out; who would be the first to shoot, who would live, who would die. Anyone in their right mind would have scarpered out of there as fast as they could. But not me; the drugs had altered my reasoning and I was stupidly enthralled by the danger of it all.

It all ended as police sirens were heard in the distance. The two sets of gunmen slowly got back into their cars then drove off, disappearing into the adjoining streets. Before I knew it, armed coppers swamped the place; lining us all up against a wall at gunpoint until they were satisfied no one left at the scene was one of the gunmen. My drug induced state thrived on the commotion and excitement of it all, never once considering the potential danger it posed. What a messed up life I was living.

Girlfriend

Somewhere in those chaotic days, I met the girl who would eventually become the mother of my eldest daughter. We met on a night out at a rave club somewhere and hit it off straight away. She was into party drugs like me and was really good looking too, a win-win for me!

She had a flat in a neighbouring city, so I used to go over and see her as often as I could. I'd spend my weekdays based at mum's, robbing stuff and selling drugs, then with a pocket full of cash I'd head over to her place and spend the weekend there. We'd either go out to a club or stay in and get off our faces with pills and dance the night away in the front room with the music blaring out. What a great basis for a meaningful relationship! Not surprisingly, things were very up and down between us and my mood swings and jealousy didn't help either. I had such low self-esteem and a crippling insecurity that no matter what she said or did to affirm me, I struggled to accept it. We'd either be getting on great or arguing like mad.

Some weekends, a group of us would make our way to her flat, empty out our stash of drugs onto the coffee table and indulge ourselves into oblivion. On one of those nights, a lad had brought with him some ketamine, which was a brand new drug at the time. It is a horse tranquilliser but even so, I was keen to sample this new delicacy. I was warned to be careful and try a small dose first. But I didn't listen and downed the full capsule of ketamine in one. "Now we'll see what's it like," I boasted to my friends.

Concerns were voiced because the amount I'd taken was supposed to be shared by a few people. But I assured everyone I would be fine and we all got back to getting high and relaxing. I suddenly got the urge for some food, so decided to nip out to the local shop for some supplies. I felt fine until I got into the shop and stood there trying to decide what to buy. I started swaying around and felt light and dizzy, my vision started to go fuzzy and I couldn't focus on the sweets in the rack. Then I blacked out and fell into the sweet counter, knocking stuff everywhere. I recovered momentarily and tried to get back up but fell into another rack and as I fell back to the floor, crisps and sweets went everywhere and I was left slumped unconscious on the shop floor, surrounded by a sea of food, crisps and bags of sweets. The shop owner tried to pull me to my feet and throw me out of the shop but I was going nowhere. I'd completely gone under and overdosed on Ketamine.

Sixteen hours later I came around in a haze, with no recollection whatsoever of what had gone on. Apparently, my girlfriend had followed me to the shop because she had been worried about me and had seen me collapse. After getting the lads, they helped me back to the flat and had put me on the couch and left, just in case I died. She then sat with me all night to make sure I remained breathing, never leaving my side. At times my breathing became so shallow and laboured that she feared I wouldn't survive. Years later she told me that she simply sat with me, holding my head back so I wouldn't swallow my tongue, praying time and time again that I wouldn't die, "God, make him breathe" she would mutter every time I had long pauses between breaths.

The first thing I did after regaining consciousness was roll a joint! She went mad with me and pleaded with me to slow down on the drug consumption but I never really listened. I simply went around boasting about the amount of ketamine I'd taken.

One night, not long after that, we had a blazing row over something – I can't even remember what it was – and I decided to leave her and go back to mum's for a while. So I called a cab, grabbed my few possessions and waited for the cab outside. When I say my possessions, all they amounted to were a few items of clothing along with my pride and joy, a newly budding cannabis plant that I'd been growing for months. It was in a massive plant pot and stood about four feet tall. When the cab arrived I jumped into the front seat and put the plant between my legs in the foot well. The top of the plant was bent back under the car roof; it looked like I was sat in a bush. The poor driver just looked at me in disbelief. I gave him mum's address and off we went with half his view through the windscreen obscured by the plant. As we drove, the smell of cannabis skunk buds became so overpowering inside the small car that he had to open his windows so as not to become overcome by the smell. It was quite a funny sight. I'm sure he was relieved to see the back of me when we finally arrived at mum's, but he still asked me if I had any skunk for sale! So I took a couple of buds off the plant and left them on the dash for him as a tip.

Our bust-ups were never permanent and before long I was back at her place again.

Italy

One day my mate Clarky arrived to see me, all excited about a new rave scene that we just had to go to. He was waving a magazine in my face about it. Once I'd calmed him down and absorbed what he was going on about, I discovered it was all to do with an emerging rave scene in Italy that was supposed to be better than any of the clubs in Ibiza. Fascinated, I read the magazine he had thrust at me. It was called Mix Mag and was at the forefront of reporting on the music scene back then. It carried reviews on new clubs and this issue featured the new Italian scene he was all excited about. It sounded fantastic, so we went and booked some flights for the following week.

When I got home and told the girlfriend, she went ballistic. So I softened the blow by telling her it was a money making trip; I reckoned we could make a killing if we took some gear to sell, it would be easy money. She eventually relented and begrudgingly let me go.

So on the day of the flight we arrived at the airport with enough gear on us to get half the country high! We'd picked up some powder the day before, a bag about the size of a bag of sugar, and had split it between us to transport. I wore some tight cycling shorts, which kept my half firmly lodged between my legs under my manhood, and got on to the flight without any problems.

As the plane landed in Rimini, we went through the usual cheap-flight bedlam of people standing up to get their luggage out of the overhead lockers, shuffled our way to the plane door and then both froze with fear. Looking out from the plane doorway, all we could see were soldiers everywhere, some armed to the teeth with machine guns, some had sniffer dogs. We just glanced at each other. Oh my! What my 'not so bright' mate and me had failed to realise was that the airport in Rimini was a military base. But there was no going back now, so we adjusted our shorts, made our way down the steps and crossed the tarmac following directions from the soldiers.

The terminal building was full of soldiers too, some working and others looking like they were off duty. We quietly picked our bags off the carousel, which were the last ones to come out, and went over to the passport control desk to make our exit. Clarky went first and handed his passport to a rather bored looking soldier. When he looked at it, a big smile beamed across his face and he started laughing. To help you understand what this guy was amused at, we must go back a few days to when we obtained our passports. Back in the nineties you could get a one-year passport over the counter from the Post Office. You had your photo taken there, then the counter staff checked your details and if all was OK they made you up a one-year passport. Well, when we went for ours, we were both stoned and, for a laugh, Clarky put up two fingers next to his head when the photo was being taken. Add to that his 'curtains' hairstyle – a parting down the middle of his head and long straight hair down each side of his face

– he looked like Neil the hippy from the Young Ones show, he looked hilarious. At the time, the woman in the Post Office didn't bat an eyelid as she stuck his photo in the passport, stamped it and handed it over to him. We had a great laugh about it but hadn't given it another thought until here we were, stood in an airport full of gun-toting soldiers, with a big bag of drugs stuffed down our pants.

The passport guy was so amused by it that he called his mates over for a look, which panicked me. I had visions of spending the next five years in an Italian prison, but Clarky was loving it. He started re-enacting the pose for them. Then more soldiers came over to see what the fuss was about, including some with dogs. I was trying to remain calm and show no signs of panic while playing along with the fun as they passed round the now infamous passport photo. It was hilarious yet heart stopping! Here we were, two druggies smuggling cocaine into a foreign country while surrounded by at least a dozen machine gun-toting security soldiers who were too preoccupied by the stupid passport photo to notice anything dodgy about the pair of us. Maybe that photo was a blessing in disguise.

After a few minutes of this, we were waved past the desk and walked out into the sunshine. We were through! We jumped into a cab and split our sides laughing about it for the whole journey to our hotel. What a relief.

Our whole week in Italy was a complete drug fest. I must have had six hours of sleep during the week and survived on one piece of pizza and lots of ice cream. Needless to say, we came back completely exhausted after living on a diet of music, dance and cocaine for so long and 'our lass' was not amused by it all. As usual, we argued and fell out again because of it all, then made up again the following week.

Things went well for a while and then she told me she was pregnant.

Fatherhood

I was well chuffed! But after my initial happiness, all the conversations about prams, cots, baby clothes and stuff made me realise it came with a financial cost and some responsibilities that freaked me out a bit. Supporting a drug habit was one thing but the added pressure of a soon-coming baby weighed heavily on me. So I decided to get a job and cut down the drugs; I was going to 'man up' and take my responsibilities seriously.

I got a job in a metal foundry working on the furnace. Melting metal down in the massive furnace was hot and dirty work but the thrill and danger of the work kept me interested and I almost enjoyed going to work.

We needed more space, so we rented a cottage together and excitedly prepared for our new arrival. We decorated a little room in the cottage as a nursery and installed a cot, a changing table and other baby stuff. The pram and other baby bits paraphernalia then started to gather downstairs. Although I'd managed to cut down on the drugs, I still spent most days smoking dope. And if I was going to have a blow out on the pills at the weekend, I restricted it to a Saturday only. My girlfriend had stopped taking anything because of the pregnancy, and she hated me going out and getting 'trollied' (slang for high on pills), so we'd argue and fall out because of the state I came home in after a night out. She pleaded with me to stop and stay home with her, which caused more arguments. But I couldn't because I still wanted to enjoy myself and I craved the feelings of euphoria the pills gave me.

We managed to stay together until she reached full term but it was a miracle given the endless arguments we had. By the time she was about eight months pregnant, I was smoking a lot of skunkweed in the house and she would wake up complaining of terrible headaches and nausea. I laughed it off, blaming the harmless weed, but the truth was I was suffering from the same symptoms too. It went on a few days, with the headaches getting worse, when I decided to do a little weeding in the garden to get some fresh air and clear my head. I'd only been out there five minutes when I put the garden fork into the soil and punctured the mains gas pipe supplying the house; the hissing noise and smell of gas was a giveaway. The gas board came out to fix the leak and carried out a full safety check of all the gas appliances in the house. The safety check revealed that the chimney flue was completely blocked by a bird's nest, which meant that whenever we had the front room gas fire on, its emissions had been unable to get away and were coming back into the house. We were being poisoned with carbon monoxide and that's where the headaches and nausea were coming from. Man, what a close call; we could have been dead in our beds within days. Once again, it seemed like someone 'up there' had been looking out for me.

I remember the morning my girlfriend woke me up to tell me that she was in labour so clearly. "Get me to the hospital" she said with some insistence.

"OK" I replied, "but first let me organise some supplies for us." Quickly, I phoned my mate and asked him to bring me some dope over while she sat and counted her contractions. I also asked him to bring his 'missus' over because she'd had children and I reckoned she could offer words of support to my girl while I got on with rolling plenty of cannabis joints for the exciting day ahead. By the time I'd finished, we had to get a move on because the contractions were increasing in frequency. We got to the hospital around lunchtime and the nurse checked how things were going. She was rather stunned and proceeded to scolded me, "she should have been here hours ago," I was told in no uncertain terms.

Within three hours of arriving at the hospital, I found myself sat in the maternity room holding the most beautiful little thing I'd ever seen in my life. It was ten past three in the afternoon, on the 4th of February. The feelings of love and affection I had towards this beautiful little girl were just overwhelming. I simply sat and gazed at her breathing softly, watching her little chest rise and fall with every breath. She was stunning and I became totally lost in my own little world with her.

The nurse interrupted my moment and took her to be weighed and checked out. I longed to hold her again and couldn't wait for her to be brought back. It was incredible to me; I marvelled at how powerful the feelings were that I felt towards this perfectly beautiful little bundle; my emotions were so heartfelt, so pure and best of all, they were not chemically induced. Of all the highs I'd experienced in my life thus far, this surpassed them all. Genuine joy, real love, authentic feelings from the depths of my heart that I'd never experienced before. I hadn't even realised feelings like this existed.

Before long the in-laws joined us and we all celebrated together, while my girlfriend got some rest. It was a surreal experience that will remain with me for the rest of my life.

After a couple of hours of holding and hugging and kissing, I needed to pop out for a while because I had a little deal to attend to. So I made my excuses and said I would be back later in the evening to visit them.

Off I went with a large celebration joint between my lips and drove across town. After picking up a large bag of celebration drugs and plenty of pills and powders, I drove past a police car that pulled out from the side of the road and started following me. Not good! So I shot off like a mad man and was chased by the police car for miles. I finally got away from it down some old country roads but had to drive like a lunatic to escape it. If caught with all I was carrying – the drugs, plus a knife and machete that I kept in the car – I would have got four years jail and I certainly didn't want to miss going back to see my beautiful little girl.

I left it a couple of hours for things to cool down before making my way back to the hospital, nervously looking around during the journey to avoid capture. I parked at the bottom of a car park in the hospital grounds and made my way back up to the ward. I pretended the evening had been uneventful and just sat there for the next hour holding my little girl, rocking and kissing her on the head, nose, cheeks and lips. Everywhere. I was besotted with her. We called her Collette.

The three of us all returned home the next day and settled into the new 'normality of family' life with a baby, and I hated it. I was no good at this kind of 'normality'. I loved my little girl, but I was so unprepared for this new way of life and couldn't cope mentally with the responsibility my newborn daughter brought with her. The combination of not getting high on drugs and taking on new and growing financial responsibility was killing me on the inside and I just wanted to escape from it all into a chemically induced haze. But the girlfriend wouldn't let me, which caused more arguments and fights.

Truth be told, looking back I now understand that my biggest struggle to stay off of the drugs was all the past hurts and pain that resurfaced whenever I was clean or sober. I had never found healing or closure from the years of rejection and abuse I had suffered. The pain of feeling unloved, and of never being good enough, still lay deep inside me and the only way for me to escape this torment was to suppress it with drugs. Escapism was my only means of survival.

So, I wasn't a very good dad at all. I soon learned that having a love for someone is not good enough on its own; it must be accompanied by practical acts of responsibility. I did try my best but the truth is my girlfriend and her family brought Collette up for the first few months while I tried to get my head around things. But I really struggled and would sneak off to get high any time I could, which always led to more fights and arguments between us.

Because money was tight, I started getting more involved with the drugs again but this time moving them around. A mate and me started making good money by moving shipments from A to B for people. The amounts we carried averaged one hundred grand in value, enough to make a good wage but not too much to get sent down for too long a term if we were caught.

The people I kept company with through all this changed too. Many of them were gangsters, which made me nervous. They were the kind of people who would shoot a person dead for fifty quid; you didn't mess with them.

Driving around with guns in the car became the norm and despite my street reputation growing increasingly worse daily, the reality was that I was scared, way out of my depth and couldn't see a way out of it.

Things at home hit breaking point just before Collette was one year old. I was spiralling out of control again and couldn't cope with the pressures of family life. I was moody, insecure and jealous of anyone and everyone. I'd had enough. No amount of positive affirmation from my family could alter my own feelings of inadequacies and inferiority. So to get away from it all, I went off to the Glastonbury festival. I told 'our lass' it was to "clear my head" but we both knew that wasn't going to happen in a hurry!

When my mates and me got there, we pitched our tent and immediately put our money making plan into action. One of the lads knew a security man who patrolled the perimeter fence of the site and made a deal with him. He agreed to turn a blind eye while we helped people climb over the high fence to get into the festival free. Well, it wasn't totally free, as they had to pay us a fee for getting them in there. Within two hours we had made about a grand and split it between the security guy and ourselves. We climbed over the fence and went inside to enjoy ourselves.

The first thing we did was to find someone with pills and we pretty much bought all he had. I bought ten and I took them all within the space of four hours! I can't remember anything of the next two days. I just remember waking up, curled up in a blanket around a campfire that some hippies had made by their tent. Apparently I'd been with them for two days, completely off my face and had amused them all in my trashed state. Some of the women hippies had looked after me and kept me safe until I finally came down and slept the drugs' affects off. When I was able to walk, I thanked them and went to find my mates and stumbled into the camper van we'd travelled in. They'd been worried sick about me, they said, but actually they expected nothing less outrageous from an idiot like me.

When I got home, it was clear my head hadn't changed one jot! 'Our lass' and me argued for two full days and enough was enough. It was over. I had to go. She couldn't cope with my behaviour and I couldn't cope with the 'family man' thing. So, I left the next morning, torn between the love I had for my family and my utter inability to be responsible. The pain of leaving Collette behind was particularly excruciating. I was devastated.

Brown

I knew of only one way to alleviate my pain, ecstasy. So the next night I went to a club but somehow, it didn't work as I expected. Although I could feel the effects of the drug, I could still feel the deeper pain. So I took another pill, and then another until I'd taken nine or ten in the space of two hours. The deep pain wouldn't go away. The promise of happiness was hopelessly false.

For six hours I lay on a sofa in a rave club without moving. I was in anguish and wanted to die. I just wanted the pain to go away. I couldn't cope with being separated from my daughter, but neither could I cope with the responsibility of being a dad. The lingering pain of separation was the last thing I felt as my head hit the pillow each night and the very first thing on waking in the morning.

I was in a state of complete turmoil and depression, and my best mate realised it. He picked me up and took me out a couple of nights on the trot, later promising he that had something for me.

"Oh yes? What is it?" I said, not really interested.

"Try some of this," he said, holding out a small paper wrap to me.

"I don't want any," I sighed and stared out of the window.

"You don't know what it is," he smirked.

Now he had my attention.

"Open it then and see," he whispered.

I unfolded the paper and looked at the light brown powder lying neatly inside the fold. It didn't look like the powders I was used to seeing; it was different in colour and texture.

"What is it? I inquired suspiciously.

"Brown" was all he said.

I knew that "brown" was the slang word for heroin and, normally I would not have touched the stuff. Over the years I had known people who'd got caught up on this 'gear' and it had not ended well for them. But by now any resolve I had left, against using heroin, had gone. I had no resistance left to fight the battle going on in my mind between my desire to suppress the pain and face up to any potential consequences. Suppression won the day.

"How do you do it?" I asked quizzically, handing it back to him.

Then the lesson began. He took out a small piece of tin foil the size of his hand and poured the powder from the paper wrap onto the middle of it. He then took out a bank note, rolled it up and put it in his mouth. Next he held a lighter flame underneath the foil until the powder began to heat up and melt into a dark brown, treacle-like lump. Then the lump began to give off smoke, which he inhaled through the tube in his mouth. He inhaled the smoke deeply and sat there motionless with his eyes closed. Holding the smoke in his lungs.

I watched him, waiting to see his reaction. The smell from the burning stuff was disgusting. He finally exhaled and opened his eyes, smiling slightly, looking at me but almost through me. His eyes glazed over. The car filled up with the smoke from the 'gear' that he had exhaled, which smelt hideous and caused me to gip. So I opened the car window to let some fresh air in.

Then he passed me the tube, in a very slow and calculated way. I took it from him without saying anything, placed it between my lips and waited, transfixed and intrigued by it all. He held out the foil and repeated the procedure of heating up the heroin. As soon as the smoke began to rise from the surface of the foil, I inhaled deeply through the tube, more, and more, until I couldn't take in anymore. My eyes began to close slightly as I held my breath and my head moved back and rested on the headrest of the car seat. I held the smoke in until I needed my next breath, then exhaled. "Again, I said, and within seconds, we'd repeated the procedure.

As I exhaled, the paper roll dropped from my lips as I tried in vain to say something and I slumped back into the chair with my arms drooped at my side. My surroundings suddenly disappeared from my thinking, as did my mate. I had no thoughts to think and nothing to worry about. It was as if I had been laid in a little box full of cotton wool and a lid gently put on top. Darkness surrounded me but I was too far gone to be afraid. The pain had stopped.

6

Dancing With the Devil

I HAVE no idea how long I sat in the car, unable to move due to the overwhelming influence of that first inhalation of heroin. But after a while I began to open my eyes and tried to regain my focus.

I couldn't. The drug had me completely paralysed by its power; I couldn't move at all. No other drug had ever made such a deep an impact on me. It wasn't just the obvious physical affect it had on me, it was the way it affected me internally, in my mind and my emotions. My mind was completely blank and I was unable to conjure up any thoughts, none whatsoever. I wasn't even aware of my surroundings; where I was or what I was doing. It was like I became completely devoid of all my human senses: sight, sound, smell, touch and feel. I was totally empty in mind, will and emotions.

Reflecting back on this, the most frightening thing about the state heroin put me in was that it removed my human ability to fear. Fear would normally take hold of me on the inside and jolt me out of such an induced state. But fear itself seemed to have been swallowed up by the power of the drug and all logic and reasoning with it too.

The only way I can explain this to people who have never taken heroin is to think about having a general anaesthetic for an operation. You lay on the bed, the anaesthetic is pumped into your body and you close your eyes. When you open them, the operation is over. It doesn't matter how long the operation has taken, it is as if you closed your eyes and opened them again straight away with nothing in the middle. But in that time your body has been cut open, parts removed, repaired or replaced and then you've been sewn back up. And you never felt a thing or thought about anything while you were under. You felt nothing and knew nothing, even though your body was put through severe trauma. That's the closest comparison I think I can make.

Whilst under the influence of heroin, I was still alive, yet I was dead; dead in my mind, will and emotions. I was alive but wasn't living; I was just existing. Yes, I was breathing and blood was still moving around my body, but my emotions and will had both shut down and ceased to work. It's a kind of self-induced coma.

So, considering all I have just explained, why did I continue taking it? Simply because it stopped my pain. I was able to exist without experiencing the real impact of my past hurts, traumas and insecurities. All feelings of hopelessness were covered in an instant. No more pain, no more sadness. Even the hang-ups about my receding ginger Afro disappeared in that sublime moment and I was at peace and rest. But it didn't last.

Heroin covered all the negative feelings and emotions inside me temporarily, but it was not able to remove them. And they all came rushing back the moment the drug wore off.

Chasing the dragon

After I came round from that first experience and gained enough focus to remember where I was, I glanced over at my mate and smiled as he opened his eyes. "Wow. That was mad," I exclaimed. "Have you got any more?" I asked. He passed me the foil and told me to try it myself this time, so I repeated the ritual with a little guidance from him. The trick was to 'chase the dragon'. When the brown lump is heated again it liquefies and begins to move or 'run' around the foil. The knack is to 'chase' this moving liquid while it gives off its smoke with the tube in your mouth, hence the saying 'chasing the dragon'. I had it mastered in no time and soon slipped back into that temporary state of bliss.

I woke up the next morning and struggled to sit up in bed. I couldn't even remember getting home and still felt very numb inside and a bit hazy. It was a good hour before I felt able to climb out of bed and start my day, and I felt the after effects of the drug long into the day.

Later that evening I thought to myself, 'I need to get myself some of that,' and without the slightest comprehension of what I was getting myself into, rang my mate to get myself supplied.

Suddenly the bad reputation that heroin had was dismissed from my mind. I had always sworn that I would never touch it or be around people who used it because it was a dirty drug that junkies used and then robbed old ladies to fund their habit. Yet there I was seeking more, having only had it for the first time the previous night. For years I had resolutely told myself that I would never even go near the stuff, but there I was, taking the first tentative steps into a heroin fuelled nightmare that would last for years and nearly cost me my life.

After splitting up with my girlfriend, I moved in with a mate who lived close to the foundry where we both worked in Leeds. We got on well and often went sneaking off together to smoke dope and get stoned in a corner of the factory somewhere. I used his spare room as my personal space and paid him some rent, usually in the form of drugs. So in the space of a few days my life had changed dramatically. I had left the family home, separated from the missus and my daughter, and was now shacked up in a mate's spare bedroom, with dope and heroin as my only real companions. I was hurtling towards rock bottom but still had a way to go.

I soon slipped into a new pattern. I would work through the week and then see Collette at the weekend, which I always looked forward to. It was complicated by the acrimonious way my ex and me had split up: basically we couldn't bear to be in each other's company. So it made me seeing Collette even harder and caused me pain that I'd never known before. It was excruciating to be away from her and to make matters worse, I blamed myself for not being good enough or able enough to be a good dad. So my own long-held belief that I was inadequate and inferior spiralled into new depths of despair. It was all very depressing and the only comfort I could find was my beloved 'gear', my heroin. And so I'd spend the day working and the nights getting stoned to escape the reality of my predicament by floating off into the 'brown' fields of the abyss.

Within a couple of weeks I was hooked and it began to affect my ability to work quite alarmingly. One day I had an accident at work while still high from the night before; I spilt some molten metal I was moving and burned my hand on some of the one thousand degree hot metal. I spent the night in hospital and lost my job later that week when my drug addiction became known.

Having lost my job, I decided to move back to mums, which she wasn't too happy about. But what mother would see her son out on the street? Certainly not mine anyway. It was back to stealing and selling drugs again to earn money, to pay for my smack habit.

I had started buying one ten-pound bag at a time, which would last me a couple of days. But by the end of the first week I needed a bag per day to keep me comfortable, and then a couple of weeks later I was on two 'tenner' bags a day.

When I look back on those days and reflect on how quickly my life completely fell apart, it still staggers me. But what I've realised is that my life didn't just collapse in an instant, things had been building up to that moment for many years and the final separation and loss of everything I held dear was just the event that triggered it all. I'd not been paying attention to the constant stream of negative choices I had been making for years, and the backlog of things I had never dealt with or brought closure on, had built up around me. This is what I call the process of my life's decline.

The process of my destructive choices over time, led to the final event that caused the collapse of the most important part of my life. And I couldn't see any way out of it. Rather than try to stand to my feet and slowly put the pieces of my life back together, I simply gave in and succumbed to the belief that I was a waste of space. I messed up everything that I did and my life could never amount to anything. I felt that I couldn't rely on anyone and I certainly couldn't rely on myself. However, in the 'brown' I'd found something that would not let me down and would always be there to sooth away the pain. But it didn't stay like that for long.

I was addicted to the 'gear'; I no longer lived but heroin lived in me, and once it had found a resting place in me through my dependency on it, heroin's offspring came and made their home in me too: hopelessness, shame, guilt, condemnation, despair and depression, to name but a few. I felt like a puppet on a string and the puppet master was called Heroin, directing everything I did and thought, directing my motives, desires and values. I had simply stopped living and now just existed. I was well and truly 'F***ed up'.

Addict

I was twenty-three when I walked back through the door of mum's house. All I had with me was a couple of black bags full my stuff, which I took upstairs and dumped in the room that I was sharing with my younger brother, who was sixteen by then. Mum's hubby, Chris, wasn't happy about me being back in the house at all. They both knew I wasn't right in myself and I suppose Chris didn't want me bringing trouble to the house like I had done in the past. But mum had the final say, so I settled in and just gave Chris a wide berth.

And so my life as an addict started. I got up whenever I woke up, or whenever my withdrawals kicked in and roused me into action. My whole day would then be spent in pursuit of heroin, looking to relieve the painful withdrawal symptoms. I wasn't interested in food or polite conversations with the family; all I was interested in was getting on the phone to find out where I could get some 'gear'. Then I'd be off out of the door, destined for some dodgy, grubby house where I could buy it, plonk myself down on some dirty sofa and begin my ritual.

Usually by that point, my withdrawals would be affecting me badly. I'd be sweating and shaking so much that someone in the dealer's house would have to help me put the powder on the foil so I didn't spill it. That stuff was too precious to spill.

It may be helpful for me to explain something about my experience of withdrawing from heroin before I go on. Once I had become addicted and was using it continuously, as soon as the effects of the drug began to wear off my body would begin to crave it again. The craving started small, with subtle signs to begin with, but then they grew in intensity and aggression. First I would get flu-like symptoms, a runny nose and aching body, followed by sweating, shivers and cramps, all of which increased in painful strength the longer the withdrawal went on. The stomach cramps and aching joints made it painful to move around. Gradually the pain would increase to such a level that it felt like every cell in my body was screaming out in pain. More, more, MORE, they would screech, tormenting both mind and body until I got to the point where I would simply do anything and everything to get my hands on some 'gear' to stop it all.

I had started taking the stuff to alleviate my emotional pain but now I was in more pain than ever. I was a young lad who should have had the world at his feet but there I was, curled up on a bed or a crummy old sofa in agonising pain, sweating and crying out for help. I had been reduced to a snivelling wreck. All the time I could hear the call of heroin at the back of my mind, shouting, "come take me and I will help you; I can stop the pain". Heroin had promised me everything, but given me nothing, but more pain.

Yet I needed it. I needed it to stay alive, at the very least to exist without pain. So I would take one big breath and fill my lungs with the poisonous fumes, then another breath, and another until the withdrawals would begin to subside and eventually stop. For a few seconds or maybe a minute, I would feel completely normal – no pain, and not on a high, just normal. Then the next intake of smoke would kick in and its powerful effects consume me completely. Followed by another lungful, and another, until my eyes would close and I would be unable to inhale anymore. I was completely under heroin's influence and out of control. My head would flop forward, tin foil in one limp hand, a lighter in the other and the tube hanging out my mouth. There I would remain until I came round and had the energy to inhale again, which I would do, until the 'gear' was burnt out. That could take up to an hour, depending on the quality of the 'gear'. Sometimes the quality of the 'gear' had been diluted, or 'cut', by other crap added by the dealers to make it go further.

This went on for weeks, the same routine just a different day. The only thing that changed was my money source. I knew I'd be OK for the first couple of days after my benefits money came through but after that I'd have to start stealing again. Shoplifting, burgling, selling stolen goods or any other idea I could come up with to make a few quid, became the focus of my day until I'd made enough to go and buy my next fix. Then it was back home to my room where I would inhale until the 'gear' was gone, and then the process would begin again.

My health began to deteriorate because I was permanently under the influence of heroin. I hardly ever ate or spent time showering and cleaning myself. Even simple things like brushing my teeth became something I did only once or twice a week. I had sold all the decent clothes and possessions I had, so I walked around like a bit of a tramp. My friendships changed and the only people I hung around with were other addicts.

Mum used to see Collette at our house every other week. So I still got to see my beautiful daughter but my addiction dictated the quality of the time I spent with her; that is if I spent any at all with her. If my withdrawals kicked in I was out of the house in an instant to get more 'gear' and a fix. If my daughter had gone by the time I returned, I just went to my room. And that was it. Even so, I did enjoy the limited time I spent with her while I was an addict. But as you would expect, my mum never trusted me to go very far with her – the shop or the park was about as far as it went – because to be perfectly honest, I couldn't be trusted to be responsible with her. It was as simple as that.

Trouble with the police inevitably follows this kind of lifestyle too, so I was regularly up in court for any number of petty charges: shoplifting, stealing cars, being in possession of drugs and so on. Usually, they led to a fine and the constant extension of my Probation Order. The funny thing about my Probation Order was that it was originally imposed for a two-year maximum period, after which I was supposed to be back on the 'straight and narrow'. Whereas, I managed to be on it for thirteen straight years because of the court extensions. I got to know the staff quite well at the Probation Office!

Digging

Even though more than twenty years have now passed, I can still remember my first injection of heroin like it was yesterday.

When I first began smoking the stuff, the high would come on quickly and last for ages. But the more I became dependent on it, the longer the effect took to come on and the shorter the period it lasted. To overcome this, some of the lads I knew injected it and were always telling me to go for the ultimate high. But I was having none of it; and I was scared of needles anyway.

But one particular morning, a good friend and me were up in my room 'chasing the dragon' when we got onto the subject of injecting. Pharmacists were now giving out clean 'digging kits'. 'Digging' was the slang word for injecting yourself with a needle, so called because you dug around under your skin with the needle looking for a vein. This helpful service provided by pharmacists removed the threat of disease from using dirty needles, which impressed my friend and I. So we made the very 'mature' decision to try it for ourselves. Smart move? I think not.

So off we went to the Pharmacy and came back clutching our very first 'digging kits'. Then we set about laying our stuff out on a little table in preparation for our first 'dig'. We'd both seen it done enough times to be confident we wouldn't mess it up.

I laid out a large metal spoon and poured some of the brown powder into its bowl to which I then added a small amount of water. Some citric acid crystals were then added which, when heated, break down heroin so it mixes with water. I held the spoon in both hands, trying to keep it as steady as I could, while my mate held a flame underneath the bowl of the spoon until the water began to bubble. Transfixed, we watched the process like a couple of witches making up a magic potion.

I slowly put the spoonful of brown, clear liquid, down onto the table. As the mixture cooled, it clarified further and we looked at each other with a mixture of anticipation and dread. But no amount of dread was going to stop us from carrying on. Into the liquid I placed a small cotton filter, like the ones used in cigarettes. We each, then, picked up a syringe and placed its needle tip on top of the filter and began to draw up the liquid into the barrel of the syringe until full. We both breathed out with relief, rather chuffed that we had managed to get this far without losing any of the precious liquid.

Off came my jumper and I applied a tourniquet around my upper arm, until the veins popped up in it. Now I was ready; so was my mate. We'd agreed we would do this together, but I was scared of needles so he popped the needle into my vein for me. I felt the prick as it broke my skin and winced. He then drew back the plunger to make sure he was in the vein and blood began to fill the barrel confirming he was. So I took the syringe from him and waited while he repeated the process on himself. There we both sat, with needles hanging out of our arms, ready to synchronise injecting ourselves. I released the tourniquet from my arm and began to push down the plunger. I watched as the brown liquid disappeared into my arm, pulled out the empty needle and waited.

Almost instantly the rush of the 'gear' hit me so hard that I slumped backwards onto my bed. My eyes closed and before I knew it, I was consumed and overwhelmed by the powerful drug. I don't know how long I lay there but when I did finally come round, my mate was still out cold. I checked if he was still breathing and then lay back down to continue enjoying the effects of the drug. It had been so intense and so overwhelming that there was no way I was ever going back to smoking it again. I was now well and truly dancing with the devil.

Little did I know at the time but the thing my mate had just done to himself for the first time, would be the very thing that would kill him. He died a few years later from an overdose leaving behind a beautiful wife and daughter. So tragic.

So now I was what is described as a 'main liner', that is, someone who injects heroin directly into their own veins. For the next couple of weeks I had to get people to pop the needle into my arm for me because I was still scared of needles. But I soon learned to do it myself; I had to, because I wasn't always with someone who could help me.

The downward spiral of my addiction continued ever deeper, as the amount of stuff I injected kept increasing. Moving into selling heroin was the natural next step for me. This was my life now and I had to make more money than ever to pay for my habit. I went to work for one of the suppliers in Leeds. It basically worked like this: I would have a driver who drove me around in a car all day while people could call the phone they gave me to place their order and arrange a safe place to meet up. We would drive there, hand over the goods and take their money. Simple.

It was well organised; we even had proper opening

hours that governed when the phone could be switched off and so on. We sold from a car simply because we were able to be constantly on the move, changing our routes and meeting places so as to avoid capture by the police. We even changed the car we drove around in every week and changed the mobile phone monthly, in another attempt to keep one step ahead of the police. The other benefit of mobile selling was to avoid being put under surveillance. People who sold class A drugs from a house or 'static' position tended to have their door kicked in by the police within a few short weeks, so mobile selling was the only way for me.

My mum's house did get raided a couple of times over the years, usually when I got caught with drugs on me or police intelligence suggested I was a dealer. But because I never sold heroin from the house, they couldn't kick the door in and the only place they could search was my bedroom because I was just a lodger. They never found anything in my room except used needles because I kept my main stash in the fields behind where I lived and I always carried my personal stash up my backside to avoid being caught with it.

I sold heroin like that for the next four years. At times I had to take a break for a few months because the heat from being caught by the police got too intense. But because I'd made tons of money selling, I enjoyed the time off and being free from the fear of arrest. I'd just laze around, getting high, and then when the money ran out, go back into the thick of it and start selling again. I could easily sell three to four thousand pounds worth of 'gear' on a good day, which was handed over to the dealer at the end of the day. He then paid me in 'gear' and cash, so I was well happy. The only thing I had to do was avoid being arrested, which was not the easiest thing to do when you're smacked up all the time.

The lad I first started selling the 'gear' with was quite a character; he was as daring and extreme as me. Not long after we had started selling together, Jay, as I'll call him, got a short jail term for a burglary he had committed a few months previously and I carried on the 'business' until he came out, after which we carried on where we'd left off. However, he'd made some promises to friends he'd made inside, and one of them was to sort them out with some 'gear'. That meant getting it inside the prison somehow.

The prison in question was a semi-closed one, which simply means that within the high and secure perimeter fence, the inmates are free to move around, as opposed to being in separated wings like I had experienced. So, one evening we turned up around seven, while the inmates were on 'free time' after evening meal, scaled the high fence using something we had brought with us and dropped down into the prison grounds. I followed Jay as he led me carefully across the prison grounds to the cellblock where his mates were waiting for us. After laughter, hugs and jokes at the expense of the prison system, we settled down to getting high on the heroin we had brought with us. At one point the 'screws' who came around doing the regular headcount almost caught us. We managed to squeeze under the beds just in time before the 'screw' popped his head around the door to count the lads in the cell. All I could see were his boots in the doorway from my hideout under the bed and I quietly laughed to myself thinking what he would do if he knew there were two extra people in that cell tonight!

Once the screws had gone and the coast was clear, we made ready to get out of there before the jail was locked up for the night. After leaving some 'gear' with the lads in fulfilment of Jay's promise, we made our way out of the cellblock and across the grounds under cover of dusk. We scaled the fence in the same way as we had got in and dropped back down onto the grass outside of the fence. Laughing, we walked back towards the car, mocking the prison system all the way home. I know people 'break out' of prison but to 'break in' was just madness. I still laugh about it, even today.

The sad thing is, Jay died a year or so later. After we stopped selling 'gear' together, he got into selling crack cocaine for some big hitters from down south and ended up smoking more of it than he sold. As a result he ended up in major debt and his suppliers threatened to take it out on him and his mum if he didn't pay up. He didn't have the money and couldn't get it, so he hung himself. Another tragedy. His mum was doubly devastated because just prior to that his other brother had been given a six-year sentence for selling crack, so she had one son in jail and one in a grave.

We went to the funeral to pay our respects, where we saw his brother who had been allowed out of jail for the funeral. He was handcuffed to a couple of 'screws' for the service and was then whisked back off to jail as soon as it was over. Later, we all met up and had a hit of heroin to honour him. How twisted and weird was our thinking.

Impact

Jay wasn't the first person I knew to die from the effects of drugs and he certainly wasn't the last.

Shaun was my first close friend to die of an overdose.

He was from the village I grew up in and was a bit younger than me, not even twenty. At the time, he was living in a caravan in his mum's back garden because she had kicked him out of the house for nicking stuff from her. He had been on the stuff for about a year when he decided to get off it and, with the help of a detox programme; he had managed to stay clean for two weeks. To celebrate being clean, he decided to celebrate with a bag of heroin and half a bottle of vodka. His mum found him dead in the caravan the following morning. More tragedy.

Hearing that someone had died from an overdose, or in a few cases had chosen to commit suicide because of their massive drug debts, became a regular thing. It was such a waste of precious lives.

The full impact of addiction extends far beyond the users; everyone connected to them is affected too. Long prison terms given to dealers and users that I knew had very negative, knock-on effects for their families. I saw children removed from their family homes and placed into the care of social services because their parents were addicts. Too many beautiful and well-educated young women were reduced to selling their bodies for sex, just to pay for their heroin habit. Others were kicked out of their homes because they or their partners had spent the rent money on 'gear'. An addict's innocent family members were often freaked out when nasty people turned up at home brandishing knives and guns, looking for the addict who owed them money. Upon not finding them they demanded money from family members, all the while holding guns or knives to their faces.

When I was selling the 'gear', people frequently brought me jewellery or stuff that they had nicked from their mums and dads to fund their drug habit. Soon afterwards I would get a call from a parent asking me if they could buy an item back because it had sentimental value as well as financial value to them. I was always happy to sell something back - for a profit of course. What a mess for those poor souls.

At other times I had women approach me who needed a fix but had no money. It didn't matter if they were married or not; they would do anything to get a hit and normally offered their bodies in exchange for a fix. Most of the time I did not take them up on it because I was high and heroin suppresses your sex drive. However some of them were stunners and it would have been a crime to say no!

The impact of heroin addiction totally consumed me. My life was completely messed up, beyond words. I hardly got to see Collette; my relationships at home were strained to breaking point, so much so that my brother couldn't cope with me so he moved out to live with his girlfriend. I was constantly on a high or constantly depressed, my health was shocking; I was underweight and malnourished. By this point my addiction was literally killing me.

Over the years I had tried to break my addiction on a number of occasions with the help of a medicated detox. I tried methadone programmes, a lofexodene detox, even 'cold turkey'. But I never got beyond a day or so because as soon as I cut down, the pains of my past would resurface and I just couldn't cope with them. So I was back on the smack sooner than you could say 'Mrs Brown'.

Even though my lifestyle was fraught with perils and near misses, I was only arrested once for supplying heroin. A woman made a statement to the police that I was her supplier, after being caught with it on her. So the police banged on my mum's door a couple of days later looking for me. I lay in bed, knowing that they couldn't kick down the door. So I opened the window and told them my mum would be down to let them in shortly. In the meantime I put my stash of 'gear' up my backside so I'd have it with me in the cells, injected myself with a needle full of 'gear' that was ready on my bedside table and waited for them to come upstairs. In they barged, arrested me and stripped me naked to check for drugs. Then it was off to the station in the car, leaving them to search my room. They found nothing. I was interviewed and charged on the strength of her witness statement. But my driver and me admitted nothing and were bailed the next morning.

Two days later, a couple of the lads came across this woman and kidnapped her. They threw her in their car and drove around until they found me at my mate's house. All I will say is that I had a very interesting chat with her and the next day a certain witness retracted her police statement against me. All the charges against my driver and me were withdrawn at my next court appearance.

Rock bottom

The possibility of overdosing became an ever more present danger. And the first time it happened was a truly scary experience. It happened after the death of a good friend, which made me decide to get off the 'gear' for good. I decided the best way to do it was to sedate myself with valium tablets and lager, so I couldn't feel the painful withdrawals. Things went OK to start with. I'd loaded myself up on about twenty valium tablets and was sat in the pub with my mum and Chris having a drink. I could still feel the withdrawal pains but was managing them by ensuring I drank enough beer.

Then my mate arrived and told me he had got some 'gear' if I wanted some. I didn't need asking twice and my resolve melted quickly away. Off we went back to my house, with needles at the ready. Into my vein it went - Bang! I went under, passing out immediately. The cocktail of alcohol, valium and heroin was overwhelming and it looked like I was done for. My breathing dropped to virtually nil at times through the night and all my mate could do was give me mouth to mouth and pray to God for help. When I came round the next morning, I couldn't remember a thing. I simply got up, had another hit and went about my normal day. It turned out my mate sat with me all night and made sure my head was held back so my airway stayed open and I could breathe. Once again, death came knocking on the door of my life but had left, empty handed.

By this time my body was a physical wreck. I'd been a heroin addict for over three years but my intake had been so excessive that I looked and felt like someone who had been on it for ten years or more. I could easily inject myself ten times a day as well as taking copious amounts of crack and other drugs. All the veins in my arms had collapsed and disappeared a long time ago. So I had moved around my body, using any vein I could find until they too collapsed. Thighs, fingers, neck, calves, top of my feet and then the tiny veins in the arch of my foot – Ouch - these used to sting. I even injected into my manhood once but made a bit of a mess of it and had internal bleeding due to a vein being torn. My manhood went black and purple, and swelled up like a big aubergine. It was weeks before it returned to normal. That meant the only accessible veins I had left were my main arteries. I spent over two years injecting into the one passing through my groin and made a bit of a mess of it in the end.

Another time I nearly overdosed, was at a friend's house. We were sat at his dining room table after his mum had gone to bed, so we 'cooked up' the heroin and injected ourselves. Within seconds my head slumped forward and landed on the table. That's the last thing I remember until I woke the next morning to the sound of his mum shouting at us. He'd slumped in his chair and had fallen onto the floor where he remained all night and I was still sat in the chair with my head resting on the table. I had not moved all night either. What I didn't realise was that my forehead had landed on the handle of the spoon, so had been resting on it all night. When she saw us both like that she freaked out; needles and spoons everywhere, small bags of heroin laying around and us two barely conscious. I got out of there as fast as I could and left him to explain things to his mum. But I was still so under the influence of the heroin that I walked into the nearby park and simply lay down and went back to sleep on the floor; I couldn't make it to the bench. I had a long bruise in the middle of my forehead for weeks afterwards.

Surviving in that messed up chaotic lifestyle became a skill in itself. In fact, looking back, I am amazed how ones survival instincts take over, even to the extent that new skills are learned way beyond those required for normal living. I learned to duck and dive from the law, to find money, to lie and cheat, to bully people and even how to extract opium from poppy flowers. I became so good at it, I could extract opium from the flower and transform it into a form that I could ingest and get my heroin hit. I got to know exactly which gardens, in which villages grew the poppies and each year I'd be there to collect the stuff when the buds were ready.

Honestly, my life was a total 'F***-up' and I was being completely overwhelmed by the darkness that enveloped every area of my life. I was nearing rock bottom.

It was entering the shadowy world of gangsters that finally took me to rock bottom. For years I'd been handing over large amounts of cash to my dealer, which I resented, so decided to start selling myself and keep the profits. That meant getting the heroin direct from the lads in Liverpool, a world that soon began to scare me. They were total gangsters. It was a world where guns and extreme violence was the norm. I'd go to pick up my 'gear' and the place would be strewn with guns, or I'd arrive there and someone would be tied to a chair in one of the rooms being beaten to a pulp. This was the norm for these lads but not for me.

I started to get paranoid about the situation and kept looking for a way out, but I was in too deep and sinking ever deeper. I would spend my evenings cooking up cocaine to make crack cocaine, in dirty stinking houses and then go dropping it off to be sold by the runners. This felt way out of my league.

Two of the lads that I knew, who sold drugs, had a massive blow out one day on the crack cocaine and when they needed some more, they put a money-making plan together. They took sawn-off shotguns and went out looking for anyone in a car. They stopped a random guy at a set of traffic lights and jumped into his car. Pointing the gun to his head, they demanded he take them to a bookies across town where one of them went inside and robbed it at gunpoint. The innocent guy was the getaway driver! They thought they had got away with the money initially, but got caught later on that day; they forced the driver to take them to a crack house; in they both went to buy crack and the driver screeched off, straight to the police to tell them everything, including where he had left them. The armed squad were straight round and caught them. They each got thirteen years for that stunt.

Lads like these were my companions in this dark and dangerous world of drug dealing. And I was done. I wanted out. I couldn't cope with it all. I had hit the bottom of my reserves. Unless I got out fast, I knew it was going to kill me.

"God please help me get out of all this," I muttered to myself as I drove home one night. "God, please help me if you can," I said a little louder, looking upwards to the sky, hopeful that God might even hear me.

"God help me!" was the last thing I remember saying before the car spun out of control and plunged through a fence and into a tree.

7

The Rock at Rock Bottom

I CAME round and tried to orientate myself. The only thing I knew was that I wasn't on the road, so I scrambled out of the car, which had its front end completely smashed in, and grabbed my stuff and walked off. The car was stolen anyway, so it wasn't a big deal to me but it probably would be to the farmer who would find it in the morning.

Then it dawned on me that I wasn't hurt; I didn't have a scratch on me. I couldn't remember anything about what had happened, except that one minute I was on the road and the next in a field with the car crunched up against a tree. Now here I was walking off as if nothing had happened - strange.

The next morning I woke up feeling very depressed; I was depressed about everything in my life. It was a complete shambles and I needed to pack it all in. So I phoned my supplier in Liverpool and told him the 'heat' was on me from the local police and I needed to lay low for a while. He was cool with it and told me to give him a ring whenever I wanted supplies again.

However, I still had my existing stock of 'gear' to sell - that became my next problem. The police knew I was selling; they had just never caught me in the act. Then one morning as I got ready to go out, I saw a police car parked outside the house. I went out and asked them if everything was OK. To my amazement they told me straight that they knew what I was doing and that they were there to stop me doing it. Wow! Talk about 'in your face' tactics, now I couldn't even go out of the house without being followed. Looking back, it wasn't such a bad thing because it gave me the perfect excuse to stop selling completely and use the remaining 'gear' I had for myself. I made a couple of phone calls to a mate of mine and basically handed the lucrative selling business I had built up to him. I was out of it.

So there I was sat at home with bundles of cash and a large bag of smack. Well, it wasn't as good as I thought it would be. Most days I was alone and began to sink into depression, plagued by spiralling thoughts of hopelessness. My doctors tried to help but to be honest; they couldn't do much for me. They could never prescribe anything to alleviate the feelings of hurt, pain, regret, guilt, shame and a whole bunch of other negative emotions that lay beneath the surface of my addiction. Each time I tried to come off the 'gear' these feelings would simply resurface, making me reach for the heroin to suppress them again.

As I mentioned earlier, I had tried many detox programmes over the years but could never get beyond doing them for a few days because the pains from my past resurfaced to strongly for me to deal with. I felt totally debilitated. Slowly my bag of 'gear' dwindled, as did my cash, until I was soon close to being back on my arse again.

I eventually reached such a low point that I started to nick things out of the house and sell them, which mum and Chris soon got fed up with. In all the years of my addiction

I had never done that before but I was desperate, so would sneak downstairs in the middle of the night, pick up anything of value and disappear into the night and wait until the dealers were open and then sell them the things I had nicked in exchange for 'gear'. Chris got so pissed off about it that he and mum decided to lock me in at night. He put two metal bars over my bedroom window, fixed to the outside wall, which only allowed me to open the window a fraction – just enough for me to throw out my roll ups. Then he put two big bolts on my bedroom door that could only be opened from outside. I was back in prison in my own home! Each night I would be locked in my 'cell' where mum and Chris knew I couldn't nick anything from the house and they could get a decent night's sleep. I had a plastic waste bin in the corner as an emergency toilet and lived like that for months. It was like being back in Armley jail again.

Seeds of hope

Then a couple of really weird things happened. Firstly, my brother Johnny who was a Christian and had been for many years, suddenly started appearing at mums again – or maybe he had always been coming around and it was just that I was now home, so noticed it more. Anyway, whenever I saw him he would tell me that God loved me and could help me if I asked him to. That would mess with my thinking and I'd always fob him off with some smart answer. But he was persistent! And every time he came round he mentioned it.

Secondly, I found out that my daughter's mum had started going to a church in Bradford, a neighbouring city to mine. I was a bit bothered by it, so called Johnny to ask if he knew what the church was like because I didn't want her getting involved in a cult or something strange with my daughter. "The church is a good one" he assured me, followed by, "do you want me to take you to check it out?"

"No way" was my quick retort.

But by then we had got into what, for me, was an uncomfortable 'God conversation'. Yet his next statement really got me thinking, "how about going into rehab then? I know a Christian one where they don't charge you money to go either".

My curiosity was engaged so I allowed him to tell me all about this Christian rehab called Teen Challenge. It was down in South Wales somewhere and offered a one-year programme of rehabilitation. The thought of getting out of my current place and away to somewhere fresh was very appealing, so I told him I would give it a go and he started the process of trying to get me in there. After some form filling and phone calls, I was given an interview date and when it arrived my mum, Johnny and I made the long drive down to South Wales.

On arrival, we had a look round and the whole place had a real sense of peace and stillness about it. I met some of the resident lads and some of the staff, and then had the interview. I thought it was going well until the conversation moved on to my heroin habit and how much I was taking. At that time I was still on six or more bags a day, which was the stinger; I was told that they had no detox programme so I would have to get off the 'gear' myself before I could be admitted. I was gutted.

Every time I'd tried to get off it before, I'd failed. So what chance did I have now? The long drive home was very emotional for me because I badly wanted to go to the rehab place but there had no idea how I could ever get off the 'gear' myself. I was confused and disappointed but the seeds of hope had been planted in me.

Soon after that, Collette's mum started dropping Collette off at my mum's every other weekend and as soon as she saw me, she would start telling me, "God loves you too". I was getting the 'God stuff' from all sides now, so always did my best to put people off before they got started with sayings things like, "I'm too far gone", or "I'm in too much of a mess, even for God to sort out" - if he was real of course!" I felt quite smug and was quietly pleased with my ability to shut them up.

In the end I told my brother, "You don't know what I'm going through and neither does God". The final ultimatum that I uttered to my brother was along the lines of, until you can show me in the bible where Jesus was a heroin addict and able to relate to my problems, then I'll listen. Until then, shut up and stop telling me God loves me.

As I began seeking real solutions, something else dawned on me that I hadn't really given much thought to before but now found myself thinking about often. Whenever I went to see doctors or drug workers, they always tried to be helpful and understanding but the bottom line to me was that they had no real idea about what I was going through or what it was truly like to be an addict. They clearly didn't know what it was like to stick needles into their bodies every day or live with the traumatic anguish and pain of withdrawals. So they spoke to me as if they were reciting a textbook on the subject and then expected me to agree with them, do what they asked and 'hey presto', I would be fine. Bullshit.

My money had run out by this point so I was back into stealing, selling stuff or borrowing to fund my habit. One day a mate and I took a long journey to get the 'gear' we needed and by the time we got to the supplier I was hurting bad; my 'rattle' (slang for withdrawals) had really kicked in. We got the 'gear' and headed off to find somewhere we could have a 'dig' because we couldn't go in the supplier's house. The more we walked around hunting for a place, the more I got fed up and frustrated because the 'rattle' was hurting so much. Then I saw a phone box, pointed it out to my mate and in we squeezed. We pulled out our spoons and put them on the little black shelf and began cooking up our 'gear'. My mate looked around a bit nervously because it was a glass phone box but I told him to shut up and get on with it; I was hurting too much to care. I finished 'cooking up' and loaded the needles and we were ready to go. I unbuttoned my jeans and pulled them down a bit, lifted up the edge of my boxer shorts and plunged the needle into my groin artery.

"Stop what you're doing and come out with your hands in the air," was the next thing I heard. I stopped and peered through the dirty phone box glass to see two police cars and four coppers standing outside with truncheons in their hands.

"Out now" screamed one of them at me.

I glanced at my mate but he didn't even look up, he was concentrating on putting his needle into his arm. Then over his shoulder I noticed a big group of school kids standing watching us with the school building just behind them.

"F*** me" I said to my mate "we're bang outside a school."

"Out now" came the scream again.

I looked down and the needle was still sticking out of my groin. I'd been stood there all that time, looking around with my trousers down around my thighs and a needle sticking out of my groin on full display to the watching school children. I grabbed the syringe and pressed down on the plunger, pushing the heroin into my blood stream while throwing a smile at one of the coppers. 'They can do what they want now,' I thought, as the effects of the heroin took hold of me.

"Come out with your hands on your head - Now" screamed a copper standing at the phone box door. I just stared at him with eyes that were beginning to glaze over.

"Got it" my mate said, as he pushed the 'gear' into his own vein.

"I'm off out then" I said, and opened the door.

As I walked out with my hands on my head, the coppers encircled me and the last thing I remember was seeing the school kids staring at me before I blacked out.

When I regained consciousness, I found myself lying in the road with my head over a drain. I tried to move but soon realised I was handcuffed. So I tried to get as comfortable as I could and waited. My mate later told me later that a copper had hit me over the head with his truncheon from behind and knocked me clean out. Well, it was that or the 'gear' that put me down and whichever it was, it left me with a massive gash on the back of my head. Then it was the usual routine - police station, interview and so on before being let out on bail charged with possession of class A drugs. It was a big story in the local paper featuring photos of local residents standing outside the phone box with arms crossed looking very angry. I didn't care.

A couple of weeks later I got stopped by the police whilst driving a car into town. I was gutted because I was still banned from driving but only had a few months before my three-year ban was up. Off we went to the police station again, this time I left with the charge of driving whilst banned and without insurance. I was given a date to appear in court two weeks ahead. When it came, I borrowed my mate's car to drive to court but got stopped by the drug squad at a traffic light because they recognised me in the car. They searched the car and me and did the usual checks, which revealed I was banned from driving. I was arrested. At the station I told them I was due in court right then so would they notify the court so I wasn't issued with an arrest warrant for not turning up?

"What are you in court for?" I was asked.

"Driving while banned", I replied. They looked at me astonished.

"So you were driving to court while banned, to appear for another charge of driving while banned! What were you thinking?" was all they could ask.

I just smirked and nodded my head.

Eventually my new date at court came round and I knew I was in a bit of trouble this time. So I had been to see my probation officer, Liz, who was preparing my pre-sentence reports for the hearing. Liz had been my caseworker for the previous eight years, so I knew her very well. The difference this time, though, was that I finally stopped the pretence and told her more about my real life. I told her more in that hour than I had done in the last eight years. It actually felt good to get some stuff off my chest and I saw her again the next day and opened up some more, and then the next. I saw her every day that week. I don't know why

I opened up to her, other than I was at the end of myself and had no fight left in me to keep up with my street cred.

Pouring my heart out to Liz left me with massive tensions in my emotions. On one hand I felt relief and freedom, but on the other, feelings of great vulnerability and weakness. I just couldn't cope with the tension and eventually ceased to care. I sank into a depression that seemed to have only one resolve - suicide. To my hopeless mind, it was the only realistic route to finding true rest and freedom from the horrible mess I was in.

At the end of the week Liz told me that she'd get on with the pre-sentence reports and give me a lift to court the following week, all I had to do was keep myself out of trouble until then.

In the days that followed, my depression deepened, and was compounded by a simple incident. So simple, I should have killed myself on the spot had I had the guts to do so. I was sat under a tree in a park one late summer's afternoon, waiting for a lad to bring me some 'gear'. I had my jumper and coat on and was shaking a little, feeling cold and achy with the 'rattle', and was taking in my surroundings. It was a warm day so plenty of people were out and about. People were sitting around on the grass chatting; other family groups were running around enjoying ball games in the sunshine. Dogs were being exercised by their owners and in the distance an ice cream van was supplying the happy children while dads kicked their footballs around. It was a scene of normal people enjoying everyday life, just doing the simple things together but in a meaningful way. The scene shouted normality, simplicity, laughter and joy, by contrast, there was me, hunched up, 'rattling' away under a tree, wrapped up in my big jumper and coat but still freezing cold; trapped in the bondage that heroin brings.

No one noticed me that day but I noticed them. And as I watched, it dawned on me what I had forfeited for my pursuit of drug-fuelled happiness. I could have been one of those happy dads. Instead, look at the state I was in. The enormity of what I'd lost weighed heavy on me as my thoughts turned to Collette. 'I wonder what she is doing now?' I mused. Then my thoughts drifted to the baby I had abandoned without ever seeing, and the one that had been aborted. The dark clouds of depression deepened around me and I felt so oppressed that I struggled to breathe. Any remaining fight or resolve left in me was sucked out in that moment and I wept quietly at the mess I was in. I just wanted to die. At least the pain would then stop.

My 'gear' finally arrived and I sneaked into some nearby bushes where I could 'cook up' and have a 'dig'. I went home and simply laid in bed until the next week – not literally of course – I went out to get some stuff everyday but then went straight back home and to bed. I didn't want to live anymore.

God Again!

One morning I woke up and was in real pain from the withdrawals and couldn't even muster up the strength to go out shoplifting. So I came up with a plan to go to the A&E department at Leeds Hospital, plead being suicidal and hopefully get some drugs from there. Mum didn't think it was such a good plan as they could section me under the Mental Health Act but I didn't care less. As long as I got some medication, I didn't care if they decided to lock me up in an asylum.

So off we went to the hospital. First a nurse saw me and I gave her my best suicide speech. She then told me to wait in a separate room until a psychiatrist was free to see me. He arrived about fifteen minutes later and after some initial greetings, sat down in a big leather chair and adopted what I thought was a very professional posture: legs crossed, hands gently holding each other on his lap and head slightly tilted to one side, looking at me intently as if he cared. But in my mind he was already trying to decide which category he could fit me into from those he had learned about in his academic training. I gave him the same speech that I had given the nurse except I wore an even sadder face and shuffled my feet in an effort to portray myself as a desperately lost heroin addict on the brink of suicide.

After my best efforts, I stopped talking and mentally patted myself on the back for what in my mind was an oscar winning performance. The psychiatrist continued to look at me intently, and all the while I wondered what drugs he would now offer me. I fidgeted a little to continue my facade until, after a short pause, he gently spoke and astounded me by what he said.

"Have you ever thought about turning to God for help with your problems?"

I just gawped at him. "You can't say that to me," I mumbled.

"I didn't come here to be preached at, I need help," I continued.

But he simply reiterated what he had said and sat there smiling at me. I was well confused by now. I simply got up in a huff and walked out, without saying another word to him.

As I walked through the hospital grounds, my thoughts were in a spin as I replayed what he had said to me. God this and God that, I bemoaned. First my brother, then the ex and now this jumped up shrink! I'm sick of all this talk about God. I was so angry because I hadn't got any drugs out of him; then add to that the God talk. 'I'm sick of it,' I thought. 'F***ing Christians'! I sulked all the way home.

Despair and dysfunction were my daily rations. Yet looking back from where I am today, in the midst of all the chaos there were glimpses of humour that still make me laugh today. I remember mum once bought me a new blue duvet set for my bed because the old one was ripped and full of cigarette burns. I went to bed that night and as inevitably happened every night, I woke during in the early hours suffering from the early stages of withdrawal – shaking, shivering, aching and sweating – I had my usual midway through the night injection, then drifted back into a heroin induced sleep. The next thing I remember was being woken up by mum. She was shaking me and screaming for me to open my eyes, her face awash with panic and fear. I was startled out of my sleep and hurriedly tried to make sense of what was happening. Why all this panic? Were the police outside, about to bust the house? I sat up and through my haze saw Chris stood in the bedroom doorway, just in his boxers, looking as frightened as mum.

"Are you ok?" She screamed at me.

"Shall we call an ambulance Chris?" I was utterly confused about the reason for all the panic and tried to ask what was going on. But mum just ignored me and kept firing questions at me without waiting long enough for me to answer. Some would say that's a bit like marriage that one! Chris stepped forward and looked a bit more closely at me, turned to mum and said, "It looks like dye".

"What do you mean?" mum asked, never taking her eyes off of me. Then in an instant her demeanour changed. The look of panic became a frown and she slapped me squarely round the face.

"You f***ing idiot," she shouted and stormed out of the room.

It turned out that I was covered in blue dye from the new duvet cover. That's what you get when you buy stuff from a cheap market stall and use it on a seriously sweaty heroin addict. When mum first saw me she thought I was blue, because I was dead! To this day she fails to see the funny side of it, but I thought it was hilarious; and still do.

My court appearance day arrived and off I went with Liz, my Probation Officer, to find out my fate. I genuinely expected a jail sentence and stood in the dock expecting the worst. When the judge asked for my probation report to read, I was very surprised to see that Liz herself stood up and asked if she could speak directly to the court. Liz explained that she hadn't written the report as she felt that she could only effectively communicate my predicament to the court verbally. The judge asked her to proceed. She went on to tell them about all my existing problems in addition to the historical issues I was still struggling with. She accepted that a custodial sentence was the only option for the court and that she anticipated this would be the outcome. Liz voiced her fears that prison could be the end of the road for me, and sat down. Wow! I wasn't expecting that.

To cut a long story short, I wasn't sent to jail. The judge said that in his many years as a magistrate, he had never had a probation officer come in person to do what she had done that day. What's more, he had been so impacted by it that he had chosen to take her opinion into account over the recommendations of the justice system. I was astonished and walked out of court a free man, save one additional probation order and an extension to my driving ban. I was so grateful to Liz taking the time to do what she did, something I will never forget.

I was well chuffed to be free again and celebrated once I got home in the only way I knew how; a needle full of 'gear' into my groin.

... And Again

Sometime after that, my brother came by the house on one of his drop-in visits and said to me, "You know you are always saying that I don't know what it's like to be an addict, so I've no right to talk to you about it?"

"Yes" I said, wondering where this conversation was going.

"Well" he said, "If you come with me to an event I'm off to in a couple of days, I'll introduce you to some guys who have been where you are right now but have been free from their addiction for years now."

He said it a little too smugly for my liking. He then continued, "And they can try to help you, if you'll take it."

"What, now?" I said alarmed.

"No, not now, on Friday night," he clarified.

He went on to tell me that Teen Challenge had a travelling group of lads who did presentations at churches and schools around the country. It was a mix of some media pieces, a few Christian songs and then the lads told their life stories - what their previous lives existed of, when they were hooked on heroin or addicted to the booze. They would describe just how they had found God and how he had set them free from a life of addiction.

I sighed a little, as the whole subject of 'God' was getting a bit boring now. I could hardly refuse him though, he was right, in that I had always used the "You don't know what it's like" card. Now my brother had come up with the goods, he knew some people who apparently did know what it was like on the other side. "OK, I'll go" I told him. Although I had in mind to use the opportunity to get some money out of my brother. After all, I couldn't possibly go if I was 'rattling', could I?

So when Friday came and he arrived to pick me up with his wife, Joanne, I was well 'rattling' and told him I would only go if he got me some 'gear' to calm me down. He was having none of it because he said I'd be so high that I wouldn't listen to anything anyone said. As a compromise he said he would give me some money on the way back. I tried every manipulation tactic I knew but he was too smart to fall for them. My only choice was to endure a two-hour church service and then I'd get a bag. It was better than nothing.

Johnny also insisted that my other brother Jeremy came along too, just in case I tried to make a run for it. To add to my shame, I was made to take off my trainers and wear some luminous, bright green flip-flops so I couldn't make a run for it. The indignity of it; talk about kicking a man while he was down!

It was Friday the 2nd of October 1998, a wet and cold

evening. We arrived at the church in Leeds just after seven and the building was already pretty full of people milling around. I sidled in nervously, flanked by my two brothers and very conscious of my bright green flip-flops. To add to my misery, I was 'rattling' and hurting so bad that I could hardly concentrate. All I could think about was getting through this ordeal and buying some smack on the way home.

We sat high up in the balcony; me being placed strategically between my brothers. It was just as well because I couldn't sit still due to the painful withdrawals and I was constantly moving trying to find a comfortable position for my hurting body to rest in, muttering and swearing to myself. I was conscious that I was turning the heads of the people sat around me by fidgeting so much. But if I got a disapproving look, I just gave them my best 'F*** you' look in return.

The presentation started and was quickly followed by everyone standing to sing one of the Christian songs I'd been warned about. Some folk were lifting their arms in the air; others were jigging or moving around as they sang. They certainly looked happy enough and every now and again someone would shout out "praise the Lord" or "Amen" and other religious stuff. It was all a bit weird and surreal. I did wonder whether some of them were on more drugs than me! I mean, they seemed to be high as a kite, yet I was supposed to be the one who had the drug habit. 'Flippin heck; this lot could do with some help too', I mused to myself.

The songs soon stopped and the Teen Challenge lads started telling their personal stories – not that I can remember any of them. Then to finish it off, a guy got up to speak. As he spoke, the room fell very quiet and I sensed the atmosphere in the place change. I tried to listen to what he was saying above the noise of my painful withdrawals but it wasn't easy. All I can clearly remember him saying was, "If you have a mountain in your life that you want God to remove, then please come down to the front."

Well I had a mountain – a heroin addiction that I wanted to be free from; I knew that much. I wasn't even sure this God was real or would even want to help me. I wasn't religious or a Christian person; I wasn't even a good person. So why should I expect any help from this so called 'loving God' he was talking about?

But for some reason, what the guy was saying started to make an impact on me, not so much in my mind but in my heart. Hope began to rise up within me but from where, I had no idea. It certainly wasn't from my frazzled mind. It stirred from deep within me and caused me to stand to my feet, then walk down the stairs from the balcony to the front of the church, flanked by my brothers of course, and still wearing those hideous flip-flops.

I just stood there at the front of the church, not sure what to do or what to say, feeling very self-conscious. I felt as if everyone was looking at me; my brothers, who were standing immediately behind me, the crowd of people sitting behind them, and the people on the stage, including the main speaker. I hung my head, as if to hide my shame, but from deep within me came an assurance that everything was going to be OK. I noticed my bright green flip-flops again; well, I could hardly miss them and I did smile to myself at the indignity of them. As I stood there, the cries of my withdrawals shook me from my moment of self-amusement; I was hurting badly and was struggling

165

to stay still. I kept altering my body position; desperate to find a position that would alleviate the pain my aching body was experiencing. I closed my eyes.

My head was telling me I was stupid to be stood there and that all the nice people looking at me knew I was a junkie and I just didn't belong with them. Yet the same assurance that I'd experienced a few moments earlier kept resounding in my heart. It was like I was stuck in the middle of two opposing forces; one trying to pull me out of that church and back to where I had come from and the other drawing me forward and urging me to stay where I was and embrace what was about to happen – whatever that was. It was a head versus the heart moment. My head was being influenced by my years of dysfunction, abuse, and addiction. My heart was being influenced by … I wasn't quite sure . . . . it was a gentle assurance, like a whisper but with great authority; a whisper I could hear even over the wretched screams of my withdrawals.

I felt a hand touch me on the shoulder and I looked up to see who it was. There stood a guy who smiled and politely motioned for me to move with him over to the side of the room where we could talk. I was relieved to be away from the front of the church but on the other hand I didn't know where I was going with him. But that same inner assurance kept telling me it was OK to just go with the flow and follow him. We sat down together on a couple of chairs and he introduced himself as Pete and asked me how I was.

"How do you think I am?" was my slightly cynical response.

He didn't react to my cynicism but simply asked me if he could tell me his story of how he used to be a heroin addict many years before; I looked at him and nodded.

He told me how he had grown up in Islington, North London, where he had gone on a journey into soft drugs, leading to hard drugs until he became addicted to heroin. He described some of the painful situations he had ended up in because of his addiction and some of the pain he had caused others. Then he began to talk about God and how he had been set free from his life as a drug addict over ten years ago. He'd then gone on to build a great life, got married, had a son and was now running a new business.

I stopped listening after a while, even though he continued to tell his story, because I became transfixed by the way he spoke about God. All this God talk usually put me off but Pete spoke about God very differently. It was like he really knew him, in a personal and intimate way. I'd never heard anyone talk about God in such a passionate and confident way before and it was so appealing to me. This guy was different. So I gave Pete my attention once more, as I fidgeted around in my chair trying to remain comfortable, and began to pay attention to every word he said.

Then came the question, in Pete's broad cockney accent, "Have you ever given your life to Jesus and asked him to forgive you of everything bad you have ever done?"

"I did it once, I think, when I was a kid and went to church," I replied.

"Did you understand what you were doing?", he pressed. "Looking back, what do you think was happening when you asked Jesus to forgive you all those years ago?" he went on.

"I really don't know," was my resigned answer.

So he began to talk about how Jesus would forgive me of every bad thing I'd ever done in life if I simply asked him to. He explained that this was possible because Jesus had died on a cross a long time ago, to pay the penalty for everyone's sin – the bad things they'd done – including mine.

This wasn't completely new to me. I had heard it before in church growing up and more recently from Johnny. Hearing it from Pete had a different effect on me. For starters, I respected him simply because he knew what I was going through because of his past life experiences. But he also impacted me because of the genuinely passionate way that he spoke about God.

"Do you want to ask Jesus to forgive you and invite him to come and live in your heart?", was his next question. He asked with such compassion and love that I immediately nodded in agreement. My head was still telling me it was all nonsense but my heart was simply exhilarated at the prospect of doing this. I knew the kind of person I had been and all the bad things I had done over the years and I knew I needed forgiveness – lots of it. But I didn't know it in my head; I knew it from my heart.

So we prayed a little prayer together and I invited Jesus to come and live in my heart. I asked for forgiveness too, lots of it, and then a bit more for all the bad stuff I'd forgotten about just to make sure everything was included. And that was it.

My brother then appeared and took a seat with us. We chatted some more, mainly about Teen Challenge, the charity for which Pete worked. I told him the story of applying for a place there a few months ago, and my frustrations about having to get clean from the 'gear' before I could be accepted. The conversation finally tapered off as the meeting had long finished and the place was almost empty by that time. So we said our goodbyes and I made my way to leave the building.

But then I stopped, turned around and went back to find Pete at the front of the church.

"Hey, what do I do now?" I asked him. "I'm still a smack head and I'm going to die if I carry on," I almost pleaded.

In my thinking I had just asked Jesus to forgive me and to come and live in my heart but it hadn't altered my current situation as I saw it. Receiving forgiveness and an assurance of going to heaven was an exhilarating prospect but was I now supposed to live out the rest of my life in the pain and misery of my addiction? How did all that work? So many questions!

Pete simply asked if he and a few of the lads could pray for me, which was all a bit alien to me, but I consented and even though I felt very self-conscious again. Four or five guys gathered around me and I stood in the middle of them feeling a little foolish, if I'm honest. Then they began to pray. As they prayed, my brain went into overdrive again telling me it was all rubbish but the assurance I now had in my heart rose up again, with even greater authority this time and I felt reassured as the negative thoughts in my mind began to dissipate.

Physically I was still withdrawing and was in a lot of pain as I stood there but then the strangest thing began to happen. The only way I can describe it is like this; from the very core of my being, a force or power that I can only describe as peace, began to invade my whole being. Every cell and fibre of my being was permeated with it, and then it filled my mind and my thoughts. As this was happening, I can clearly remember the painful withdrawals stopping, almost in an instant. Then, the painful feelings from my past that had held me in emotional and mental bondage for so many years were simply swallowed up by the peace that now enveloped me from the inside out.

I knew there and then that I had just experienced the love of God. It was as if a divine exchange had just taken place; God had taken away all the addiction and pain that had held me in chains and in exchange had given me the peace and rest that my heart had been yearning for all my life.

While all this was going on, I didn't have any visions of angels on clouds playing harps, or saint Peter standing by the pearly gates; I simply experienced the supernatural love of God that broke my addiction and swallowed up all of the pain. In that moment of time, I knew from the bottom of my heart that God was so real and so alive, that it transformed me in an instant.

From that moment on, over seventeen years ago now, I have never desired drugs, had cravings for, or taken heroin. Neither did I suffer from painful withdrawal symptoms the days following that nights meeting. It was a miracle. I had found the rock of God's love when I was at rock bottom in life. I have never been the same since.

God set me free from my crippling addiction to heroin, in that instant, without any further need for a medicated detox programme. That night I returned home and quietly went to my bedroom 'cell' where I slept peacefully for the first time in years.

I was finally empty of drugs; instead I was now full of Jesus.

8

University of Hope

I AWOKE early the next morning, just as the first light of dawn began to illuminate my bedroom. Out of bed I jumped, desperate for the toilet, so I made use of the bucket in the corner of my bedroom; all the while my mind replaying the events of the previous evening. Nothing had changed externally, I was still locked in my bedroom and a glance towards the window reminded me that its security bars were still in place; but inside, I felt so alive; I was almost giddy with excitement.

I sat on the end of my bed by the window and began to roll up a cigarette. Just then, I noticed that the sun was emerging from behind the houses across the street. Its powerful rays brightened my room and I watched mesmerised, for the next few minutes as its beautiful orange globe rose slowly into the morning sky; emitting powerful rays of positive light that filled my bedroom and my heart.

In that moment, a memory came to mind, triggered by the captivating sunrise. I had been here before. Just a couple of months earlier I had woken up very early one morning, rattling and desperately in need of a hit of heroin, but mum wasn't up yet to let me out of my 'bed cell'. So I had to endure a long wait before she unlocked my door.

That particular morning I had been sitting in the same spot at the end of my bed, watching the sunrise over the same house rooves, my body writhing from excruciating withdrawal pains. In that moment of despair, I spoke to myself and told myself that I would never enjoy the simplicity and beauty of a sunrise ever again because of all the pain that I was in; I sobbed my heart out. Now that was no longer true! I had just watched a beautiful sunrise free from the influence of heroin and the pain of withdrawals - it was amazing! I genuinely believe that that sunrise was a simple, loving, gesture from God to show me that he had seen and heard my cries of despair and had responded to them with his loving kindness.

Mum finally emerged, pulled back the big iron bolts and popped her head around the door to check on me. She looked rather surprised when I flashed her a big smile and said morning to her. Her surprise turned to shock when I asked her what was for breakfast as I made my way past her to get into the bathroom for a shower. "Breakfast?" she said, "you haven't had any breakfast for years!"

I looked at myself in the bathroom mirror and was greeted by the same harrowed look that I had had for years. I was pale, very pale; almost grey looking, gaunt with sunken eyes and very unkempt. The bright ginger Afro had long since gone, been replaced with a crew cut to the sides with nothing more than a bare landing strip on top. One thing was different today - my eyes. Their familiar dark, cold and haunting stare seemed to have been replaced by something of a warm sparkle; it was as if they'd been illuminated from the inside.

As I stripped for the shower, I glanced down at my emaciated body and winced a little at the damage I had inflicted on it - four years of stabbing needles into myself had left its mark. I am not exaggerating when I say that I had injected myself over 7000 times in a little under 4 years, that's an average of 5 times a day. At the height of my addiction, I would inject myself 10 times a day. Old needle track marks lined my arms, thighs and calves. Bruises were scattered everywhere and there was not a single protruding or visible vein to be seen. Scabs and septic wounds littered my body, especially in my groin area, both sides of which were just swollen, bruised masses from the years of daily intrusions. There was even a small permanent hole in my right groin where the skin had never had chance to heal because of the continuous injections.

Faced with the reality of my physique, a wave of panic swept over me and I found myself thinking, I'm still an addict, I need heroin – fast, before I start withdrawing. My brain slipped into autopilot, instinct kicked in, I started working out where I could get some gear from. 'I need to get moving,' my mind was saying. But at the same time, the confident assurance I'd experienced the night before rose up within me and assured me that I didn't need any heroin because I wasn't an addict anymore. I paused, gathered my thoughts and looked at myself in the mirror again. I had no physical withdrawal pains - check. I had no physical cravings or desire for heroin – check again. Relief flooded my heart.

Then it struck me, that underneath the veneer of the heroin-induced devastation, I was still a reasonably good-looking chap; and I flashed myself a smile. The guy in the mirror flashed one back! It seemed I was left with only memories of my heroin use and the painful withdrawals. Whatever had happened to me the night before had genuinely made me a new person, so I was now going to fix my mind on that reality, not on the memories of what had been. As I did so, I was left with a confident feeling that everything was going to be well.

After getting cleaned up and dressed, I skipped downstairs – well, not literally with a rope, just a bit more energetic than normal – and enjoyed some breakfast and quality time with mum the likes of which I had not had for years. I told her everything that had happened the night before. She was surprised, but pleased, to hear of my new found faith and to see my improved behaviour. But she was no fool and was understandably rather sceptical about it. After all, I had lied to her and Chris for years so she wasn't about take this new story as gospel truth just yet. Hence the bedroom door remained bolted at night and the window bars remained in place, but I didn't care. I now saw those bars and bolts differently; I no longer viewed them as being there to stop me getting out, I saw them as a protection against my old lifestyle getting back in.

Collette was brought over to mum's later that day and I had a fantastic time with her. We read books and did some colouring in of pictures, something I had never done before - that's a fact - the first time I had done colouring in with my daughter whilst not high on drugs. I was completely normal for the first time in her entire life. Collette was almost five by then and I had wasted the previous four years devoid of any emotional attachment to her. Now I was overwhelmed with love for her. I would start crying for no reason; I was just happy to be holding her and being with her. It was a wonderful sensation but a bit weird at the same time for me.

Collette's mum got the shock of her life when she next

saw me. I told her about what God had done for me, how he had broken the power of my addiction in an instant. There I was speaking to her about how good God was and that he loved her. Talk about turning the tables!

Waiting game

The following Monday morning, I wrote a letter to Pete at Teen Challenge, (TC) telling him what God had done for me on that Friday night and how my life had been radically transformed since then. That triggered a phone call from TC to say that now I was off the drugs, I could be given a place and I would be allocated the next available bed. I was ecstatic. Now it was just a waiting game, a 4 week waiting game to be precise.

Over those weeks I spent as much time as I could with Collette, loving her as best I could in the circumstances. Mum also used this time to her advantage and got me building a large brick shed in her back garden, as well as doing other little jobs around the house. It never included removing the bars and bolts from my 'bed cell' though; she still didn't trust me enough for that, plus she wanted to keep me as safe and secure as possible until the day came for me to move down to Wales.

Word soon spread amongst my mates, that something had happened to me and that I wasn't on the gear anymore; a number of them came over to see me to find out if it was true, which of course it was. Mum used to allow them into the living room with me, but she would never allow me to be left alone with any of them, in case they tried to slip me anything. I told my mates I had given my life to Jesus and that he had broken the power of my addiction. Most, if not all, were sceptical but they couldn't deny the truth. By then I had not touched the gear for days, weeks even, and I was clean off everything. Some of them thought I had gone mad or had had a mental breakdown due to all the drugs I had previously taken. Others thought it was probably some scheme of mine, drummed up with ulterior motives of course. A few were really pleased for me but couldn't get their heads around the God bit. One thing is for sure, they all left my mum's house with the words I had spoken, "God loves you and he will help you get off the drugs if you simply ask him," ringing in their ears.

In what seemed no time at all, Tuesday 3rd November 1998 arrived, the day of my big move to South Wales. The journey reinforced the reality of what I was doing and I had a difficult emotional time that day. I had kissed Collette goodbye the previous Sunday night and spent Monday packing my belongings into a case I had borrowed. Once the journey began and I was actually driving away from Wakefield, leaving Collette and my family behind, my heart broke. I longed to stay because I had loved every minute I had spent with them since getting clean but knew in my heart that I needed to go. I may have been delivered in an instant from my addiction, but right now my life and emotions were in a complete mess. I needed space, time and loads of support to put my life back together, so that I could become a trustworthy and reliable dad to Collette. TC was offering me the space, time and support to do this. So I set my face towards the future, wiped the tears away and quietly thanked God in my heart for the opportunity to build myself a new life as I was driven south by my brother.

Repair and prepare

I was heading for Teen Challenge, a non-profit-making international Christian charity, which it might be helpful for you the reader, to know a little more about at this point. Then you may have a better chance of understanding why it had such a positive influence on me as my story unfolds.

TC was founded in New York during the late 1950's as a Christian response to the emergence of a violent adolescent teenage gang and drug culture in the city. It was an attempt to show the love of God to those hurting souls and ever since then, its primary focus has been to reach out to all those on the edges of society. TC's message is simple: that true freedom from social, physical, mental and emotional problems can only truly be found in an intimate and personal relationship with Jesus Christ. Over the years the charity has expanded into over one hundred countries across five continents and is today, one of the world's largest, non-profit-making organisations.

TC's core programme consists of a twelve-month residential course, designed to help people who have been damaged by addictive behaviour of various kinds, develop and mature in all areas of life. Each day on the programme is meticulously organised for the participants, which at first sight can seem rather rigid, but it is a simply way of teaching the programme participants to take control of their own lives and achieve a sense of responsibility as opposed to staying passive or apathetic – which is where most of them are at when they arrive at TC. A strict timetable is followed that includes absolutely everything:- getting up, meal times, chapel, class activities, physical exercise, contact with family members and periods of free time. Yes, it is rigid but necessarily so.

We arrived in Gorslas, the house of TC, about twenty miles from Swansea, South Wales, just after lunch. After a quick goodbye to mum and my brother Johnny, I was shown to my room. I unpacked my few belongings and then met with centre manager, Mike Rankin, to go through the house rules and complete some paper work. In the process he asked me how old I was, "twenty six", I replied. Mike hesitated before writing it down, shot me a confused look, did a few sums in his head and then said, "No you're not, you're twenty seven," such is the memory of an addict! I had genuinely lost all track of time because, like all addicts, I had not celebrated birthdays, Christmas, or any other milestones in life once I'd been engulfed by the blur of endless addiction. How sad.

With the formalities completed and the evening routine navigated, I eventually went to bed. There I lay down for my first night in my new world, quietly thanking God that I was still alive and I hadn't died as an addict.

The TC home was much larger than I remembered from my first visit – probably because my head was clear this time! The building had originally been a small supermarket, then purchased, renovated and converted into living accommodation in the 1980s by a man called Reverend John Macey. John was the one who established TC in the UK and has since developed it to be the national charity it is today with rehabilitation homes up and down the country. I have the utmost respect for John Macey, who together with his wife Ann, gave their lives to building a Christian ministry that would house and accommodate men – and women in their female homes – from horrendous backgrounds and give them the love, help and support they needed to rebuild their lives.

John became, and still is, a very dear friend of mine and became like a second dad to me whilst I was a resident at TC, and during my subsequent time as a staff member. John gave me the love and affirmation I had craved all my life, but most of all he believed in me and gave me confidence; he was and still remains a constant source of encouragement to me.

The home at Gorslas accommodated twenty-two men plus resident staff. The building comprised a kitchen, dining room, lounge, classroom, games room at ground level; upstairs where the bedrooms upstairs. It was a fantastic place, very well kept, and had a large back garden too.

The day-to-day programme took some getting used to because I'd led such an undisciplined and hectic lifestyle as an addict. Initially I found it difficult to get up at a certain time, shave every day, and eat breakfast at a set time and so on. Every part of the day was organised for me, from the moment I woke to the moment I went to bed. If I failed to be where I was supposed to be at the required time, I was given more washing up duties in addition to the ones I was already on the rota to do. At first I thought it was stern and uncaring but I soon came to realise the benefits of the system; it was simply designed to teach me time-keeping skills, punctuality, discipline and consistency, as well as the practical skills I was doing.

The daily routine consisted of attending a chapel service after breakfast and classes for the rest of the morning. It was in the classes that we learned how to find true freedom by applying biblical principles to our lives. After lunch we did manual work for a few hours, which was a novelty at first, because like me many of the lads had never had regular jobs in their lives. Work duties could include a variety of tasks including furniture restoration, making concrete products or doing general maintenance and repairs within the home. We would then have our evening meal followed by a little free time before going back to the classroom for more teaching on what it means to be a Christian and related things. Then there was a bit more free time, followed by an evening drink before one last chapel service, and finally bed.

At weekends the programme was much more relaxed. We did a big house clean each Saturday morning followed by sports activities in the afternoon, then followed by a movie in the evening; something I always looked forward to. Sunday involved going to church twice, in the morning and evening, with free time in the afternoon, when I usually went for a snooze.

Time to sit and talk with counsellors and advisers was also built into the programme, which formed a crucial element in our rehabilitation. We all arrived with such a diverse range of problems stemming from our addictions; from bad debts; dealing with estranged children, pending court cases, broken marriages and a host of other dysfunctions. TC also worked closely with registered GP's and other local agencies to support of the mental, emotional and physical well-being of the residents.

Over the years, some people have criticised the TC programme for being too long, but I have fundamentally disagreed with them. The problem with detox or rehabilitation programmes that only last for a few weeks or a couple of months is that they deal only with the drug or alcohol misuse, by weaning a person off their dependency to the substance but not dealing with everything else. People with addictions have typically been living their lives of dysfunction for five, ten, fifteen or more years, so it is unrealistic to think that all the damage caused by these years of addictions can be fixed in just a few short weeks. That is the beauty and ingenuity of the TC programme: it allows time for restoration from the emotional, physical and mental damage, laying a foundation for rebuilding personal relationships again. In a nutshell, TC asked of me to give them one year of my life with my full participation, in return they would give me all the help, support and resources at their disposal to repair the damage of my past and prepare me for a new future. I saw TC as a 'repair and prepare' shop. The fruit of its work has proved their way to be an excellent one.

It took me a little while to fit into the TC routines but once I understood the long-term benefits and goals, I was up for it.

The parts of the programme I enjoyed the most were the chapel services and the Christian teaching. Although I had experienced something extraordinary at that church service a few weeks ago, I now wanted to understand exactly what had happened to me. I also wanted to get to know more about God and to deepen my relationship with him.

I had lots of questions. For example, I had heard people talk about God, Jesus and the Holy Spirit, which confused me. Which one really was God? and who were the other two, I wondered? Then, what was heaven all about? Would I spend eternity floating around in the sky with wings and wearing a nightgown ... or what? So it went on, an endless stream of weird and wonderful questions flooded through my mind, and the class times gave me the opportunity to get some answers.

My journey through life had turned me into a sceptical person. I'd become innately suspicious of people in general and I took this same scepticism into my new life as a Christian. So I didn't just believe something was true because a person said it was, I wanted to find out for myself. As a result I spent as much time as possible studying my bible and praying to God, looking for answers. I soon learned that God never disappointed me and helped find the answers I sought.

I remember times in the chapel services when the preacher asked us all if anyone needed a physical healing in their body. Lads went forward for prayer and I witnessed them receiving healing from Hepatitis C, irregular heartbeats and other chronic illnesses. I knew those lads - they weren't idiots, liars or fools. Those healings were genuine miracles, just like my deliverance from heroin had been. It was incredible to see and created in me a steely determination to seek the source of those healings - God himself.

Because I had determined that I wasn't there just for some rest and relaxation while I got clean from drugs, my time on the programme flew by. I was like a sponge, soaking up everything I could, looking to learn and change my past behaviour patterns and ways of thinking. Boy, did I have a lot of work to do - a lot to repair and a lot to prepare.

Ripple effect

As you will appreciate, my whole focus whilst at TC was taken up on getting through the processes and the daily routines. At the same time however, I was becoming increasingly aware of a ripple effect that the dramatic encounter with God was having on others in my world.

Firstly, Liz, my probation officer, drove in her own personal, time all the way down to South Wales to visit me to check whether this transformation in me that she had heard about was real. It was nice to see a familiar face from back home in Wakefield. She described how I had become the talk of the local probation service, being the first person ever in their care to get free from heroin.

Secondly, I heard from mum that about a month after I had left Wakefield to join TC, two drug squad police officers turned up on her doorstep. She told them in no uncertain terms to "F*** off" because I was no longer living at that address. Apparently they too had heard rumours about my freedom from drug addiction and they wanted to check it out for themselves. Mum told them quite smugly that the rumours were all true and how very proud she was of me. The two drug squad officers, much to mum's surprise, were elated with the news about me and expressed their hope that it would last. It was only later that I learned that they made a phone call to TC head office to check out that it was all true what they'd heard about me, and to enquire after my well-being. Who would have imagined that happening?!

My encounter with God was also the topic of much talk amongst churches in the area where I used to live, sell 'gear' and commit crime. The churches, I guess, knew above everyone else that what had happened to me, i.e. my conversion, was a miracle and they were pleased for me. I received a letter one day from someone who attended one of these churches, encouraging me to keep up with my new relationship with God………. at first I thought the letter was from some mad crazy, Christian woman that I did not know nor had ever met. As it turned out I later came to the realisation that this person wasn't mad or crazy, just very passionate about her faith and it came through in her letter to me very strongly. On returning home from TC, I met the writer of that letter, Cath, and we have been friends ever since.

The ripple effect also reached and was felt by my immediate and extended family - it was incredible. Mum had a queue of people wanting to know what had happened and whether it was true. And so the conversations went on. Many of my family members wanted to know more about this miraculous God and they started attending churches to get some answers to their personal God questions. I reckon that during my first year or so at TC, thirteen members of my close and extended family gave their lives to Jesus and experienced the forgiveness and love of God in their own lives. Wow! Thank you Jesus.

My family used to come and visit me about once a month, and brought Collette each time, which was the highlight of my month. I so badly wanted to be a good dad to her and I treasured every moment we spent together. I missed her and my family terribly each time they left after a visit, but I knew that I had plenty more work to do in myself before I would be ready to be a trustworthy dad on a more permanent basis. What I didn't want to happen was to get caught up in the emotion of missing her and then leaving the programme prematurely to go back to Yorkshire. It was tempting but I managed to resist.

A pearl of wisdom I learned early on in the programme in relation to Collette and my family, was that I should not complete the programme and turn my life around for them. I wasn't doing it for them; I was doing it for me. If I did it for me, then they would be the beneficiaries of my choices. But if I did it for them, I could well end up feeling they didn't appreciate all I had done for them and end up going back to my old life.

Forgiveness was another profound truth I learned so much about while at TC. I discovered that true forgiveness sets me free. As I have recounted in these pages, I had been a victim of some very painful experiences and I had always determined not to forgive my abusers because to be quite frank, they didn't deserve it. But after listening to some teaching about forgiveness and unforgiveness, it suddenly dawned on me that forgiving a person for something they have done to me, however bad, was not for their benefit, it was for mine. Wow! I had been holding on to bitterness, resentment, anger and un forgiveness towards certain people without any understanding that those negative feelings were having a detrimental effect on me, not them. I'd spent years inadvertently hurting myself and at times losing sleep while dwelling on the past, and all the while, the other person had not lost a single wink of sleep or been affected by my ill feelings towards them. Forgiveness was quite simply about releasing myself from the pain of a past situation, leaving it behind, giving it to God and moving forward. As long as I was looking back and focusing on the pains in my past, I couldn't move forward with my life. Forgiveness is a fundamental key towards freedom.

End in sight

Shortly after I entered the programme, TC needed some

bricklaying work doing and as I had done it many years before at college, I put myself forward. It became one of my work duties and I worked alongside an experienced bricklayer who taught me so much over the year. Eventually I got to a stage where I didn't need to be supervised and could be left to do the work on my own. That was a great boost to my self-confidence. Acquiring that skill was also instrumental in me being employed by the charity, after I had completed the programme.

As I approached the latter part of the programme, I decided to join the travelling group of lads who had spoken that night I went to church in Leeds and had my encounter with God. I wasn't the best singer in the group – well let's be honest, I was probably the worst – but I loved to tell my story to the people in the churches and schools that we visited. I was passionate about what God had done in my life and so grateful to have been given a second chance that I wanted to tell anyone and everyone about it. I spent what ended up being a wonderful year or so, travelling the country with an amazing group of lads who, like me, had been set free from horrendous life styles, by a loving and caring God. Our message was simple: there is no such thing as a hopeless situation when you invite God into the equation and we are the living proof – or 'The Evidence' as we were known.

It was such a joy to see hope enter people's hearts as they listened to us and to see many decide to give their lives to Jesus like we had done. It is an amazing privilege to see a person, once heavily burdened with the negative influences of addiction, brokenness, isolation, hopelessness and depression, begin to change. We watched people's demeanour change as they invited Jesus into their hearts; the burdens that once crippled them were being lifted and their countenance began to positively shine as the joy and peace of knowing they were forgiven and loved by God flooded their soul.

My time living down in Wales, with the Teen Challenge family had been a truly extraordinary experience that was preparing me to eventually return back to my family back in Yorkshire. My time on the programme was nearing the end, yet I was so aware I needed more time to get myself straight and to keep growing in my faith. So I decided to stay on as a volunteer once the programme was over.

Staying on as a volunteer – which I did for another nine months – meant I could continue to travel with 'The Evidence' on church and school visits; keep developing my building skills and continue to put the practical pieces of my life back together. One of my aims was to get my driving licence back so I could travel home to see Collette more frequently, although I wasn't looking forward to the prospect of insuring a car after five driving bans! I just needed to get on with it and so I did. My first insurance premium was almost three grand for a car that was worth two hundred quid!

After that, in September 2000, I went and lived in India for six months to help with building work at the Teen Challenge centre in India. The charity over there had been established for ten years. It had recently purchased a forty acre parcel of land and embarked on a six-year programme to build a multiple occupancy village that could house hundreds of vulnerable people from all areas of Indian society; young girls and women rescued from people traffickers and prostitution; young men caught up in drug and alcohol addiction; and children as young as one year old who had been simply abandoned on the streets, left to fend for themselves or die from starvation.

The programme in India wasn't as simple as the programme that I had completed in the UK because over there, neither social care nor benefits system existed. Teen Challenge India would house, clothe, feed, educate and protect every person within their care until that person reached an age or position of social maturity, however long that took. Then they could move on to live a normal life in freedom.

I arrived there when the construction process was at an early stage and lent my strengths to the team building whatever was required of me. I made some incredible friendships along the way; Bhapa, Bunti, Vinod, Lester, Bala, Santosh, Pinto, uncle Deverage and a very special friend also called Tim, to name but a few; some were staff members, some residents on the TC programme – it did not make any difference to me, they were all friends of mine.

The challenges of working in India were new to me. I had to contend with working in temperatures well over thirty 30 degrees, and get used to mosquitos, venomous snakes and scorpions, the latter I had often spotted in the grassland around the site. Then there was the challenge of working on a team where English was not everyone's first language. And the food took me a while to get used to seeing as everything was prepared with spices and chillies. The infamous 'deli belly' got the better of me four times.

However, my time in India was very special season of my life that will remain with me forever. All in all, it was a life- transforming experience and the friends I made have become life-long friends.

New life ahead

Once I had returned to the UK, I spent a further year in south Wales by joining the TC staff team. My role was that of maintenance manager for all of their properties. Although I still desperately missed Collette, the new job offered me a bunch of additional benefits that would further enhance my complete rehabilitation. For a start, I would get a P45, a major plus for someone who hadn't had a recognised job for the last ten years. In addition I got a decent salary that allowed me to start saving and my further experience in the building trade would better equip me to find a decent job once I finally returned to Yorkshire.

I used that year to increase the frequency of my visits to see Collette and also spent my holiday leave back home with her. In that way my involvement in her life gradually became more stable and reliable, which was another major hurdle that I had had to overcome to regain the trust of Mel, Collette's mum. In all fairness, I could understand Mel's mistrust of me. I'd been the one who'd never been reliable or trustworthy in our former relationship and she'd single-handedly raised Collette, so she was understandably cautious now that I was back more regularly.

I had to regain Mel's trust and I was helped in this by another nugget of truth I had learned at TC - trust is not given it is earned. I had blown any trust Mel had in me clean out of the water by my behaviour, and I couldn't expect her to give me it back just because I was a Christian and saying all the right things. I had to earn it by being trustworthy and keeping our agreements about when I'd see Collette and when I had get her back home and so on.

I also knew that rebuilding trust could take years and would be set by Mel's timescale, not mine.

Another way that I hoped would rebuild trust was by being financially diligent. I was a wage earner now so I started paying Mel maintenance money for Collette, something I'd never done before. As my income increased, so did the payments and I remained committed to those payments for the next eleven years until Collette finished full time education. I never missed a payment.

One final memory I must tell you about is the opportunity I had to join another of TC's mission building trips, this time to their centre in Swaziland, southern Africa. I ended up going there three times for about one month at a time and was privileged to partner with an amazing couple, Kevin and Helen Ward, who have built a fantastic rehabilitation centre together with homes to help people caught up in addiction, poverty, rejection and HIV. Kevin and Helen loved people back to wholeness through any number of homes that they ran their programmes through.

Kevin is to me an amazing man of God who inadvertently helped me to understand that men can love God without becoming feminine in the process. To me he modelled being a man who loved God, loved his wife and family and yet retained his masculinity in a godly way. I was so inspired simply watching him walk out his faith in God.

I think I had developed a bit of a warped perception about christian men and their tendency to be effeminate. Looking back with hindsight, it was probably rooted in my short introduction to church as a teenager when I recall thinking at the time that many of the guys lacked masculinity; they were a bit wimpy and effeminate. I was also influenced back then by the portrayal of Christians in the media, in particular the Vicar called Ashley in Emmerdale who was most certainly portrayed as a wimp. Then there was the wacky, chain-smoking, gossip Dot Cotton from East Enders. Such is the power of the soaps.

Because of those influences I had developed the irrational idea that at some point in my christian life I would have to begin behaving like them one day and tone my masculinity down somewhat. But Kevin showed me that it was possible for a man to retain his masculinity and honour God, whilst loving his wife and family too. He is one of my heroes.

In Swaziland, as in India, I relished working away in the hot sun, building wood and masonry buildings on the side of a mountain to accommodate more vulnerable people. What a great opportunity it was to experience another culture and to make yet more great friends.

My time with TC was rapidly drawing to a close, by which time I had spent three and a half years in South Wales. Reflecting back on that time now, I am staggered at the way God moulded and shaped me in preparation for a new life - it was just astonishing! Some adjustments that I had had to navigated were massive and life changing, whereas others were miniscule, made in the secret place of my inner personal world. I gained skills in practical living, people skills and emotional management skills, which thankfully stopped me running off to get high when I was tempted. My physical health blossomed and i put a few much-needed pounds on my drug battered body. I managed to rebuild damaged relationships with family and friends that I had hurt through my past behaviour and choices. I could go on and on. All the time I was guided by the steady hand of the TC staff. I will be eternally grateful to them. In fact, I could probably write another book on the dynamics of rehabilitation from my personal perspective – maybe a book for another day!

As I turned the corner into 2002, I knew I was finally ready to go back home to Yorkshire. I set about compiling a list of things that needed to be in place before I made the move. My top three priorities were finding somewhere to live, finding a job and finding a good church. The house and job requirements were pretty obvious, but finding a good church was equally important to me. I understood by then that if I was to sustain my strong christian walk, I needed a great church family around me, particularly once I was back on my old stomping ground (the areas I formerly committed my crimes). Even though I had burned all my bridges when I first moved down to south Wales, by destroying the contact details of anyone from my old lifestyle so that I would never be tempted to make contact at some point in the future; after all, it was still plausible to think that news of my return would spread like wildfire among my old mates. I had to make new friendship circles fast and I knew that the best place to do this would be around a great church that would become my spiritual home – I just had to find it.

The prospect of returning home did cause some feelings of apprehension to rise up within me and to be honest; I was a little scared at the thought of it. All I had ever known in Wakefield and the surrounding cities, was a life of crime, drugs and violence and my reputation went before me! 'Will I be able to stay away from trouble and the drugs?', I anxiously pondered. As I started to become apprehensive about these things, the peaceful inner assurance that I had grown to recognise and trust, rose up in my heart and I knew that everything was going to be OK. God had my back covered now.

I had a quiet word with mum and she and Chris agreed to let me stay with them, just until I had the chance to save up some more money to get a place of my own. A building job fell into my lap, so to speak, which I found out about through a friend who told me about a building company owner (who also belonged to a great church in Bradford) looking to take on a lad – there I was ready and available to start in a month's time. The company owner conducted a telephone interview with me and gave me the job. Happy days.

Handing in my resignation letter to TC was one of the hardest things I have ever done. The TC staff had been so supportive over the years, but I knew it was time and I had a beautiful daughter to go back to and look after, who was growing up so fast that I would miss out if I didn't act quickly. I worked my final weeks and prepared to leave the place that had truly become my home for that season of my life. I spent the evenings over the last couple of weeks saying goodbye to all of the amazing friends that I'd made and during the day, I handed over my job duties to the lad who was taking over from me.

On the Friday of my departure, at teatime I packed my car, filled up with petrol and pulled on to the motorway to begin my five-hour journey home. This was a major transition point in my life and I went through a whole bunch of emotions as I headed along the M4 that leads out of South Wales. Behind me was a season of my life that had been such a joy to live, because in all honesty, the previous three and a half years had been the only time during my teenage and adult life that I hadn't been on drugs or involved in crime.

A sense of great satisfaction warmed my heart as I journeyed on, reflecting back on my time at TC. I had accomplished so much and finally proved to myself that I wasn't a loser or a waste of time. I was a man of God with a hope and a future. So, with a twinkle in my eye and the joy of the Lord in my heart, I put my foot on the gas and headed home to Yorkshire.

9

To Love and Be Loved

I MADE the journey north alone; just me, my thoughts and all my worldly possessions crammed into the back of the car.

As the motorway miles sped by, I started to think about my old mates and wondered what they might be doing now. 'Were they still on the gear and still messed up?' I pondered, 'were they even alive?; a more shocking thought, but one that had a realistic chance of being true. That got me thinking about other friends I'd had who were no longer alive. Their faces flashed into my mind as I recalled their names; Dave, Shaun, Beddy, Chris, Charlie, Tony, Neil – the picture gallery in my mind continued – Ian, Bobby, James, Mark and so it went on. Everyone was a precious life lost to heroin; and those were just the ones that I knew had died before I went to Wales. Each of them had left behind broken-hearted mum's, dad's and other family members. Each of them had never seen the children they might have raised, had heroin had not taken their lives; generations of children that were never born. So sad.

But here I was, alive, healthy and ready to re-enter the theatre of life. 'Why had God kept me alive?' I tried to reason, 'and why me and not them', I pondered. These and a host of other unanswerable questions swirled around in my mind as I changed lanes in frustration to get around the car in front of me that was travelling far too slow for the motorway. Speeding past the car and glancing sideways noticing a female driver, I permitted myself a smile – 'I knew I was right' – "women drivers!" I whispered under my breath. "Be patient and courteous Tim", I told myself. Then I put my foot down to create some distance between us.

I was now well on my way up the M1 into the last leg of my journey. I passed Sheffield and Barnsley and started looking out for landmarks that would tell me I was almost home. Even though it was dark, the brightly illuminated clock tower in Wakefield came into view and I knew I would be home in ten minutes – back on life's stage, back in the ring.

Re-entry

I pulled up outside mums and both she and Chris came out to greet me and to help me get my stuff inside. As I took the first armfuls up to my room I paused at the top of the stairs to look at the bedroom door. No more bolts, but the screw holes and shadowy imprints made by the previous locks on the paint could still be seen. "That's in the past now," I told myself and carried my belongings into my bedroom. Within one hour I had unpacked, eaten, and was settling down for an early night, trying to imagine what my future would look like as I drifted off to sleep.

The next morning I was up bright and early because Collette was coming to stay at mum's for the weekend. I went to pick her up and a couple of hours later, after a nice breakfast at good old McDonalds, I walked into the house.

"Gary came around for you about an hour ago", mum told me with a slightly worried look on her face. "He left his number and asked that you give him a call. The number's on that bit of paper on top of the TV," she concluded.

I was stunned. Gary was my old supplier from Liverpool. 'How on earth has he found out that I'm back up here? and so soon?,' I thought to myself, as I took Collette's coat off. To this day I don't know how he found out. To come and see me within sixteen hours of getting home was bonkers!, "where's that number again?", I asked mum. She pointed at the TV. I walked over, picked up the scrap of paper, popped it into my mouth and after giving it a little chew, swallowed it. There was no way I was going to throw it into the bin where I might be tempted to go back and retrieve it later 'just in case'.

Talk about a negative influence trying to shipwreck my return! All it did was show me that the fight for my life wasn't over yet and that I needed to guard what I did and where I went closely. I told mum that I didn't know how Gary knew I was home and stressed that I had not arranged it, just to alleviate any fears she had that it was my doing. If anything, it strengthened my resolve to make the right choices, however hard, to protect and maintain my new Christian way of life in this old environment. I became a man on a mission!

The next thing I needed to find was a good church. One immediately came to mind, the Abundant Life Church in Bradford. I knew it was spiritually awake and preached a message that was very relevant - a million miles from some of the traditional churches I had been in. I had been to it a few times over the years while up from south Wales seeing family and Collette. But on those occasions I had always been like a pilgrim passing through, whereas now I was looking for a spiritual home to call my own. And I had high expectations, as I had been spoilt by a fantastic church experience during my time in south Wales where I attended Swansea Elim Church, under the excellent pastoral care of Phil and Lynn Hills who had become the benchmark for me.

I am pleased to say that Abundant Life Church didn't disappoint, it more than met my desires for a church home and I settled in there with total ease under the pastoral leadership of Paul Scanlon and Stephen Matthew. In fact I've remained part of that church family for over fourteen years now. My spiritual growth over those years owes a lot to the two aforementioned pastors, as well as my personal commitment to develop and deepen my relationship with God and remain committed to playing my part in the local church.

That was home and church sorted - next it was the job. Keith, the guy who had offered me a job working for his building company, was also part of the Abundant Life Church, so we met up one Sunday, talked a few things through and I started work for him the next day. It was that easy! That was also the start of a friendship and a working relationship that continues to today. Keith knew all about my former background, yet still gave me the opportunity to prove myself, which was a massive boost to my confidence.

Life back in Wakefield got off to a great start because of the positive choices I made and I threw myself into my work, church life and of course being a dad to Collette.

Old mates

I re-entered life carefully, deliberately trying to avoid my old haunts and neighbourhoods like the plague, except the one where I was living of course; I couldn't avoid that one. I had made a conscious decision to change my life and walk in a different direction, so I wasn't going to compromise my newfound freedom at any cost and that included my former pals. But inevitably I bumped into them, especially in my first few weeks back home.

Part of me was glad to see them; after all, they were my mates. We'd grown up and gone through school together, navigated many ups and downs together and so had bonded as friends. Needless to say, they wanted me to go and hang out with them, to have a beer in town and whatever else. I declined their invitations at first because I couldn't allow myself to flirt with the former things. My mates seemed genuinely pleased for me, saying I looked well and had done good for myself, they just couldn't understand the God bit. In their minds, I was still 'one of them' and they couldn't really understand my reluctance to hang out with them.

"Do you think you're better than us now?" they kept asking me.

"Of course I don't!" I'd protest. "I just don't want that life anymore; I've left it all behind and have no intention of going back to it," I confidently declared. Our conversations often ended a little heated and sometimes I had to just turn on my heels and leave because they wouldn't take 'no' for an answer. Doing so always left me with a tinge of sadness, because they were genuine friends. It was simply the things they were doing or taking that created the separation between us. They wanted the freedom I had found but without God. "God is the source of your freedom" I would try to explain, but to no avail. Sadly, they preferred to stay in their pit of despair rather than give their lives to Jesus and live in the open fields of grace, hope and freedom he offers.

Another tack they took with me was to say, "Tim, you've been brainwashed! God doesn't exist, it's all a load of s**t."

"No, you're wrong", I would counter, "God is real and he has really changed my life; I'm the living proof", I would confidently declare with my head held high. "Just look at me, I've been drug free for years, I'm healthy and full of hope for the future. God did that, not me!"

"You've gone f***ing mad" they usually concluded, shaking their heads at my stubborn stance.

"Mad!" I would exclaim. "Well if living free from addiction, pain, suffering and hopelessness means I'm mad, then I'm happy to be mad every day of the week," I would end up saying.

I found those early encounters very challenging, both mentally and emotionally. Sorrow filled my heart as I watched my old mates choose to remain in their addictions. I'd listen to their stories of brokenness and impending prison sentences, knowing there was an answer in Jesus. I knew there was a God who loved them so much and wanted to lift them out of their pit of despair. But my message of hope seemed to just fall on deaf ears and unbelieving hearts.

Those conversations taught me that it had been much easier to live out my faith back in Wales. Back there I had pretty much lived in a 'bubble', surrounded by committed and passionate christians. It had its advantages of course but did tend to create a siege mentality at times, a sort of 'us against the world' attitude. Now I was living well and truly in the world and had to live as a strong christian in the middle of it.

A few unsteady months followed, during which I made some daft choices from time to time. Things such as going out occasionally and getting hammered on the drink and hanging out with a girl that wasn't a christian or even interested in going to church. She had other interests in me that I eventually had to flee from! I was flirting with things that were not God's best for my life. "What am I doing to myself?" I sternly asked myself one day. "This has to stop," I warned myself, "If I don't watch it, I'll be back on the slippery slope of decline before I know it."

I had burned all my bridges when I had initially moved to south Wales but there I was starting to rebuild them again. Firstly, the brick of an old friendship, followed by the next brick of a night out with the lads. Another brick of 'I can't be bothered with church today' and another of 'I wonder what so and so is doing today?' Very subtly, I was erecting bridges back into my former way of life and it had to stop – Now.

During my time at TC I remember a few occasions when lads left the programme part of the way through, or returned home after completing the programme and then started flirting with their former lifestyle or drugs again. Some of these lads had overdosed and died, and even though I knew some of these guys personally, I was beginning to take the first tentative steps in that very same direction. Scary.

I made a strong decision to drop those choices and anyone associated with them. I didn't give myself a hard time over the mistakes I had made, I simply stopped making them, turned my attention back to God and continued to develop new friendships within the church family. What better way to do it than throwing myself into helping out in any area of church that I could find.

I also started to look for a house of my own, closer to where the Abundant life church was in Bradford, another choice to get away from my old familiar neighbourhood and so avoid the temptations that were knocking on the door of my life.

I soon regained my focus and began to look forward to my first drug-free Christmas with Collette. I had missed all four Christmases whilst at TC, being on the programme for two, then away in India and Africa for the other two. I was really excited about this Christmas. Equilibrium had been restored.

The Bombshell

I was sat in my chair one Sunday morning waiting for the church service to start, looking around nonchalantly, and there she was, walking right towards me. Wow! I couldn't take my eyes off of her. I snapped myself out of staring and gathered myself. She was a bombshell. Beautiful. Her gorgeous face and huge smile captivated me - it was divine. The way she carried herself was just so attractive to watch. I looked down and pretended to be looking for something in my Bible as she engaged with me. "Hi, I'm Donna," she said.

"Hi," I replied, trying not to blush.

"I'm looking to put a small team together to help out with a church project and I wondered if you'd fancy getting involved?" she asked, flashing her big smile at me.

I was putty in her hands by now and simply nodded in agreement. She could have asked me to clean horse manure off of the road outside with a toothbrush and I wouldn't have objected.

"Great" she said, then took my number and promised to be in touch. That was it. Off she walked into the crowd - but not before I'd had a quick glance at her bum.

True to her word, she contacted me a few days later and we met with the rest of the team to get the church initiative moving forward. Even now I can't remember what that initiative was. At the time my brain had turned to mush I was so smitten by her; all that mattered was that I got to hang out with her while working on a church initiative. We got on well together. A few project meetings later we were chatting and she told me she was going into hospital for a back operation so wouldn't be around for a couple of weeks. After a bit of innocent probing, I managed to discover her operation date and the hospital she'd be in. Then I set about hatching a plan to visit her the day after the operation - a surprise visit.

On the appointed day I turned up at the hospital, made my way along the maze of corridors until I found her room, knocked cheerily and let myself in. "Surprise!" And she was surprised. Then she came out with every woman's famous last words, "I wish I had known you were coming, I would have put some makeup on".

"Oh, you look just fine," I lied.

I made myself comfortable in one of those not so comfortable hospital chairs, ordered some coffee – it being a private hospital – and just hung around as we chatted and got to know each other a bit more. When it was time to go, I considered chancing my arm and kissing her on the cheek; but didn't. I decided it wasn't really appropriate considering she was doped up on painkillers. I left, but not before arranging to see her again once she was out of hospital.

Fast-forward a couple of weeks to the next time I saw her. It was at church one evening and she looked even better than the first time I had laid eyes on her - hot, hot and hotter! By then it was just a few days before Christmas and the church wasn't due to meet again until the New Year. I offered her a lift home just to get a little more time with her and, of course, because I am a polite and courteous christian man. When we got there she invited me in for a coffee, which I readily agreed to and she introduced me to her parents.

As I drove home later that night, my mind was working overtime on the reality of us getting together. I had lots of questions because I'd never had a christian girlfriend before and wasn't sure what I was supposed to do. What did I do next? Was I allowed to kiss her or was it only holding hands? Did we need a chaperone with us when we were together? This was way too stressful for me. In the past things had been very different; it was meet in a club or a pub, both get off our faces on drink or drugs and then get into each other's pants before we got home. Easy. But this was different and Donna certainly wasn't a girl like that; she would have smacked me in the face if I had tried anything on with her. So I just stopped thinking about it and parked up outside mum's house.

We spent quite a bit of time together over that Christmas period and I was always trying to work out how to conduct myself as a nice christian, despite the fact that I was completely hooked on her. I would invariably leave her after spending a little time together, then kick myself for nor saying something about how I felt about her. It was embarrassing; the former hard case heroin dealer had been reduced to a shy admirer whenever I was around her. What I now know is that my polite reticence frustrated her no end! So the next time we were together, which was New Year's Day 2003, she walked up to me and gave me a big kiss on the lips. "Does this mean we're going out now?" I teased her.

"Yes" was her short reply.

'Happy days,' I thought. And that was the start of our relationship.

I wish I could tell you that those first few months of us dating were all love and romance, flowers and long walks holding hands, gazing lovingly into each other's eyes. But they weren't. Simply because it was me she was going out with. Yes, we had some great times but I also put her through a lot.

When I came out of rehab, I thought I was a great christian, in a good place with God and ready to get on with life. But once I started dating Donna, my life started falling apart; or so it seemed. Not long into our relationship my old feelings of insecurity, jealousy and low self-confidence reappeared. "Where have these come from?" I would ask myself and "I was great before I met her!". It was Serious agony.

I am still surprised she stuck with me but she did. I knew I loved her but just needed some help with my hang-ups. I sat with a couple of pastors from the church and talked my issues through with them, only to be passed on to some others with more experience. They too referred me on. It was bonkers; I'd seen nearly every pastor in the church before God gave me someone in the church who had more experience and was able to help me dismantle my faulty thinking. And that someone was my senior pastor, Paul.

After five minutes of listening to me, he started talking to me about things I'd not even been asking about; I was a little confused. He explained that all the 'negatives' I had talked about were simply fruit, not the root of the problem. I was still confused. He explained the difference between a root and its fruit, using the analogy of a drug addict. The drug addiction wasn't the real problem; it was just the thing visible on the surface of someone's life, the fruit. The real problem was the thing that caused the person to take drugs, the root. Returning to me, he said that my feelings of insecurity, jealousy, low self-esteem and lack of confidence were just the fruit, the things I could see. And somewhere there was a root that was producing them; that was what needed addressing. No bad root, no bad fruit. Wow! I loved it.

Over the years I had sat with many counsellors and psychiatrists and nothing I had been told came close to Paul's insightful diagnosis. It took some time to identify all the roots - but gradually we did, and I started a journey of replacing my bad roots of guilt, regret, condemnation, with positive ones namely of being accepted and loved by God. The whole process took a few years but slowly my root thinking changed and, as a consequence, my fruit changed.

Donna was an absolute rock to me in the early days of that process. Things would be great between us for a while, then I would have a setback and go to get help. Meanwhile, Donna remained steadfast; true to herself and our relationship; and never without that gorgeous smile on her face. I must be honest, it wasn't easy for me as a man to get to grips with it; most men are afraid to even mention the words jealousy or insecurity. They'd rather pretend that these negative emotions weren't part of their lives and hide quietly, living with the negative consequences - something I did for years. Things however were beginning to change; not only did I love Donna but I was beginning to love myself. I was determined not to let the hang ups that had caused me so much heartache and destroyed every other relationship I had ever had, break this one up.

The Bride

Our Spring wedding day approached fast. We'd got engaged the previous September, nine months after first starting to date, and had already bought a house together. The house needed totally refurbishing and I spent the six months leading up to our 'big day' working through the day and renovating the house in the evenings. I renewed the roof, replaced the windows, installed new electrics and central heating, plumbed in a new bathroom and kitchen, plastered it throughout and sorted the garden out. I was knackered when the day finally came! It looked great though, so I gave myself a big pat on the back.

There I stood at the front of the church, on 27th March 2004, one of the proudest days of my life. From my vantage point, I looked at the sea of people gathering and was overwhelmed by the support both Donna and I had been shown by our family, friends and church family.

I had very little say in the wedding plans, like most men I reckon, except for choosing what I would wear and who would be my best man. The first bit was easy. I went for a grey and white pinstripe two-piece trouser and waistcoat outfit, made to measure with a white custom made shirt embroidered with our names and the date of the wedding on the cuffs. A matching cravat finished it off. I looked handsome, even if I do say so myself. Dan was my best man, another easy choice. We had met while I lived in south Wales. He lived close to the men's home and was a local business owner who supported the work of TC. He welcomed me into his family with such grace and acceptance that I felt like I'd known them all my life. Dan is a big bear-like man, with a baldhead to match mine, and an honest love for God that was truly inspirational. We both must have looked like a pair of moneylenders or bouncers standing at the front of the church waiting for the ceremony to begin.

The hall quietened and everyone stood as the entrance music began: 'There can be miracles' by Maria Carey. That was the only part of the ceremony that I had had a say in. I wanted it as a declaration to God that this day was proof, 'there can be miracles' and both Donna and I were the living proof.

The first bridesmaid to come down the aisle was my sister, accompanied by my five-year-old twin nephews in their dapper little outfits. Next came Donna's youngest sister with her daughter as a flower girl. Her older sister came next, with her two girls and then around the corner came my beautiful daughter, Collette. She was now ten and looked stunning in her little silk bridesmaid dress, hair all curled and smiling at me; the picture of perfection. I struggled to keep my composure and my lip began to quiver. I tried to cover it up with my hand but it can clearly be seen on the wedding DVD, something Donna takes great pleasure in pointing out every time she watches it with someone.

After a brief pause, the room gasped as Donna came into view, flanked by her proud dad. I just gazed at her, like Homer Simpson looks longingly at a doughnut! She wore a stunning, full length, figure hugging ivory dress. The front had a beautiful sweetheart neckline with a chiffon cowl neck running over the top, covered in small and sparkly Swarovski crystals. The chiffon arms were exquisite, medieval in style and hanging just over the top of her hands. They too were hemmed with delicately scattered shimmering crystals. The back of the dress caressed her contours, flowing down from each shoulder and meeting around her lower back where a small row of ivory buttons held the two sides in union. A diamantes hemmed ivory train trailed softly to the floor from Donna's waistline at the back which was adorned with a bow. A white flowered garland held her hair up and a simple chain and diamond pendant adorned her neck. Wow! All details supplied by Donna, you will understand, I was too busy adoring her to remember the details!

I didn't take my eyes off of her as she elegantly walked down the aisle towards me, holding her dad with one hand and clutching a single white lily in the other. The words to the song played out - there can be miracles, when you believe', as she drew closer and closer towards me. Women looked on with genuine emotion, men looked bored with genuine apathy. But what did I care; I was transfixed by my bride.

We exchanged our vows in an atmosphere interspersed with songs of worship to a loving God who had brought us together. We smiled at each other. At one point during the service, Collette joined us both at the front and Donna took a moment to make a promise to accept, love and nurture her as if she was her own. Precious.

We had a small reception at the church for our family and friends and then left for our honeymoon in the Maldives. That was the start of our lives together.

The birth

Coming home as a married couple was a great feeling and we quickly settled into married life with excitement and hope for a great life ahead of us. Donna returned to working in the church we attended and I resumed building work. At that stage I was no longer working for my old boss, I had started my own building company just before we were married, while continuing to develop my business and building skills. I began to re-educate myself in the construction trades, obtaining all my NVQ's in bricklaying before progressing onto an HNC in construction management. Altogether I spent a total of five years in further education, my aim was to become as highly trained as possible within the building industry.

One morning, just as I was leaving the house for work, Donna screamed at me in excitement, "I'm pregnant". I was over the moon and couldn't wait to tell Collette that she would be having a little brother or sister soon. Life was good for us. Donna and I would often sit and reflect back on our lives and express our gratitude to God and each other for all we had together; it was beyond comprehension compared to what I'd been experiencing just a few short years ago.

My building business was so successful that I started up a second company specialising in house extensions. My real dream however was to become a house builder and I came to regard as the pinnacle of my career; all my efforts to re-educate myself were leading to the fulfilment of that dream. Eventually I set up a third company when the opportunity came along to build my first house. I purchased a piece of land and submitted an application to become a registered house builder with the National House Building Council (NHBC), the regulatory body that oversee house builders in the UK. The process entailed them making regular inspections as I built my first house and if the work was satisfactory, then I would receive my accreditation. It went well and on completion of the build I received notification that I had been accepted on to the national register of house builders. It was such a proud moment of my life, I was now one of only seventeen thousand people in the UK on the NHBC register, which wasn't bad considering I had only been out of rehab five years and had left school with barely a qualification to my name.

After Donna had become pregnant, we decided to move to a larger house, more suited to our growing family. It turned out to be a horrendous process but we finally moved into our new home on the baby's due date! An army of girls swept in to prepare the nursery for our new arrival and my mate and I spent the afternoon fitting a new 50 inch plasma TV to the wall – priorities. Male priorities!

Chloe was born on the 20th of October, two weeks after her due date. It was a long labour during which we spent thirty-four hours on the maternity ward. I would have liked to say that I was a pillar of strength to Donna throughout her labour but that's not quite how it turned out. For a start I have a real hang up with hospitals and I'm not sure why, but they make me feel weak and faint. I sat quietly in a corner of the room and tried to remain inconspicuous as the midwives started to induce Donna. After a full day of waiting I was bored to tears and prowling around to alleviate my boredom, which frustrated Donna and the midwives so they sent me out of the way to get some food and to create some peace from me. When I got back, the nurses were giving Donna an epidural and just the sight of it made me almost faint. In the end the nurses had to stop helping Donna and tend to me otherwise I would have collapsed in a heap!

As time dragged on, my thoughts turned to the up and coming rugby World Cup final that was due to kick off at 7.30pm that same evening; England were playing South Africa. My hope was that Chloe would have arrived either before or after the game. But no, at 7 o'clock sharp a clinical decision was made that Donna would require a C-section and it would be immediately. "But the rugby kicks off in half an hour!" I stupidly protested. Silence, and four disapproving looks from the staff in the room, was the only response I got. But God was by my side because the anaesthetist had the game playing on his radio during the operation. It was a win-win situation for me, except that England lost. That soon paled into insignificance as my beautiful daughter finally arrived.

Being a parent to a new born baby was a whole new experience for me! I soon learned to survive on very little sleep, and then after about a year Donna announced that she was pregnant again. What great news, but our excitement was short-lived. Donna was rushed to hospital one morning with stomach pains and lost the baby a few hours later. We were devastated.

I was hurting, trying to rationalise it all, but my biggest concern was Donna; I simply held, loved and supported her as best I knew how. It turned out that she had an inflamed bowel that had wrapped itself around one of her tubes and caused the miscarriage. Donna remained in hospital until her bowel problem got sorted out and I, together with Donna's supportive family, rallied around and kept family life going.

It was a tough season in our lives. I had lots of questions like, 'Why did it happen?', and 'Why did God allow it or not step in to prevent it?' I tried to understand but never found a satisfactory answer to my questions, even to this day. What I can say is that Donna and I found God to be an amazing source of comfort in those dark days and we simply chose to trust him despite our lack of understanding. We took it a day at a time, relying on God to be our source of strength and found him to be our ever present, comforting Father God.

We all grieve in a uniquely personal way, and I'm not the type of person who is motivated to publicly share or offload my pain onto others in the hope that they will give me support and affirmation in return. I simply cried in private when my head was on the pillow and gave my tears to God. I didn't name the baby, write it a letter or anything like that; I simply found a place of rest in the knowledge that I would see the baby in heaven one day. That was enough for me.

Some ten months later when Donna told me she was pregnant again, we were both overjoyed but understandably a little more apprehensive as the miscarriage was still fresh in our minds. Once again, I had to dig deep into God for renewed strength as I supported my family. Days turned to weeks and we prayed daily that the pregnancy would not end in tragedy. Donna blossomed; she looked more beautiful than ever while she carried our baby. Then as she approached mid-term, the doctors decided that Donna would have a prearranged C-section.

The thought of it made me feel faint! I knew however it was important to be there to support Donna, which is what I did, and Jack was born on the 2nd June 2010 – a footballing World Cup year. Exactly ten days later, Jack and me watched our first England game together, with him dressed in his St George's baby grow outfit. Donna rested on the couch with Collette curled up beside her and Chloe played with her toys on the floor. I held Jack closely as I jumped up from the chair to celebrate when England scored their winning goal against the USA. Life was good. Yet something inside me told me my life still wasn't quite complete, not just yet; there was still a piece missing.

10

Comfort in Pain

THE first few weeks after Jack's arrival, were incredibly busy; they were filled with laughter, joy and lots of baby cries but we loved it. After being surrounded by girls for so many years, having a boy in the family was such fun and added a whole new dimension to our family life. Jack had been delivered by C-section, which meant Donna needed lots of rest in those first few weeks, so lots of our friends pitched in to help us in practical ways. One friend in particular was invaluable, a dear friend called Sarah who was living with us at the time while waiting for her own up and coming wedding. Sarah helped Donna with Jack, took Chloe to nursery and did whatever else needed doing around the house while I was out at work. She was a legend and we couldn't have got through those first few months without her.

In the busyness of our lives, I began to sense something wasn't quite right. "Donna just doesn't seem to be right," I said to Sarah one day. "I can't put my finger on it but she just doesn't seem herself," I continued thoughtfully. Sarah agreed with me and between us we put it down to the after effects of the caesarean operation, a new baby, and being generally tired. I was wrong and it would take a while before things became clear to me.

Jack was three months old when Donna fell and broke her left ankle, an accident which slowed her recovery down no end. Donna had almost returned to full mobility again before this so it was a big setback. Families rallied around us, like they do, and I decided at that time to close one of the businesses down so that I could spend more time at home.

Unbelievably, four months later she fell over in the kitchen and broke her right ankle. Only this time the ankle dislocated as well, requiring an operation to correct it with pins and plates. Once more, Donna found herself in a cast and back to square one in terms of her mobility. This placed further stress and strain on us as a family. I was feeling under pressure keeping the business running alongside my family responsibilities, which became too much for me to cope with, so in the end I decided to close another company in order to spend as much time as possible at home. I soon found that it was extremely difficult to keep enough money coming in to pay the bills while juggling things at home.

To make matters worse, five months after Donna's last ankle break, I broke mine in an accident at work! It was now me who was sat at home unable to work; it was tough. The blessing in the midst of it all was that because I was stuck at home, I noticed how oddly Donna was behaving. As a result we went to the GP together, where she was diagnosed as having severe postnatal depression. This explained to me why my once happy, smiley wife had been reduced to a shadow of her former self and was struggling to cope with herself, let alone the kids. Despite the much-appreciated help of family and friends, she simply couldn't cope and was sinking into a pit of despair.

My initial response was one of anger at myself for missing the early signs of Donna's illness. I had been so busy at work that I had left her to deal with the kids and her broken ankles pretty much on her own - with help from family and friends of course. I was also confused because I didn't really understand the illness. I also had fundamental question; one of which was, we were christians and therefore not supposed to get depressed, so what was going on, because the reality was that Donna was ill.

Returning to work was out of the question for me once I understood that Donna was struggling alone with the kids because of her illness. So I had no choice but to close the last company down and become a 'stay at home dad', on crutches to begin with!

I can't lie. That season of our lives was a massive struggle and I often wondered if we would ever come through it. Sarah had long since moved out and got married, so there I was looking after our two children and my sick wife on my own. We had no money coming in and didn't have much in the way of savings because business had been tough since the economic downturn of 2008. What we did have ran out very quickly - I resorted to living on credit cards and ran up large debts. I felt very alone during those dark days and all I could do was try to forget about my own feelings and concentrate on Donna and the kids. Night after night I pleaded with God to help me stay sane and give me the strength for just another day.

The events that unfolded in our lives that year shook us to the core. Everything had been turned up side down; it was chaos. I was under mental and emotional pressure I had never experienced previously and our marital joy and laughter had disappeared. I was racking up debts in an effort to survive and all intentions of good household stewardship went out of the window. I just couldn't keep all the 'plates of responsibility spinning' and one by one they began to crash around my feet. The house was in a mess, letters remained unopened, clothes only got washed when there was nothing else in the wardrobe, I forgot to tax and MOT the car, and the list went on. The only 'plates' I couldn't let drop were Donna and the kids. That was it. Even my relationship with God was reduced to nothing more than a frequent cry of God help me interspersed with expletives out of sheer frustration. I was at the end of myself.

If ever there was a time in my life when I might have been tempted to return to the heroin, this was it. But I never contemplated it for a second. At times it felt like God simply wasn't listening to my prayers because I didn't get the immediate answer I wanted. But he was listening, and he helped us, just not in the way I was expecting.

Friends in need

The relentless pressure took me almost to breaking point. It was then that I got a phone call that turned out to be the tipping point towards change.

The phone call was from Jay, Director of TC. Jay called me to touch base and to chat about the major relocation plan the charity were in the middle of. The plan was to relocate their male residents and head office from South Wales to the Midlands the following spring. I had been previously aware of these plans and had been seriously thinking about getting involved in some way. As we talked on the phone, the pressures I had endured over the last year or so, and supressed inside me, simply overwhelmed me and I just broke down in tears. I told him everything that was going on at home, about the postnatal depression, the broken bones, the debts and everything else. He said very little, just listened. Then he told me everything was going to be fine and asked if he could call me back in half an hour? "Of course," I said and he hung up.

When Jay called me back, he simply said, "We would love you to bring Donna down to the women's centre in Wales where she can stay with us for a month". Jay went on to explain, "she wouldn't be part of the programme" he continued, "We'd just like the chance to support and help her. She can stay with the female staff and help around the place. How's that sound?" he concluded.

I just cried again. Relief filled my heart. A weight was lifted from my shoulders and I felt like I could breathe freely again for the first time in months. "When?" was about the only thing I could mutter in response.

"Tomorrow if you want," was his unexpected reply. And that was settled.

We hurriedly put some childcare arrangements in place before Donna and I set off on the long journey down to South Wales. Donna looked so frail as I glanced over at her sat in the car beside me. I knew that God had made a way for this to happen. He was leading her to a green pasture where her soul could be restored and my heart was filled with peace.

That month that Donna spent helping out at TC was truly transforming. Just being in such a God-centred environment was crucial for her healing, as she was encouraged to look again to Jesus as the one who would bring her through to a new place of health and wholeness. And God didn't disappoint.

While Donna was away I carried on with life. I had some thinking and breathing space, so set about getting the house back in order; opening and responding to mail, getting the car taxed and MOT'd – both of which were six months overdue – and doing whatever else was needed. More importantly, I had some personal breathing space now I could rest assured Donna was in a safe place and I was able to regain some mental strength of my own. I installed some routine back into family life and a sense of stability returned; we ate meals together regularly and kept to regular bed times together. Peace returned to the house.

Everyday the children and I prayed for Donna; God always gave me an assurance that Donna was safe in the palm of his hand, and would be well again. The postnatal depression affected Donna in ways far beyond what it is appropriate for me to mention in these pages. Suffice to say, that is Donna's story to tell one day, if she so wishes.

We had a small welcome home party when Donna returned home, more for the kid's sake than ours, but it marked the moment. I quickly saw the evidence of change in her. She had the air of her former self again and was smiling a lot more. Her language was much more positive and she even spoke optimistically about the future and the possibility of sharing her story with others one day. Wow!

In case I am giving you the reader a false impression, let me just say that Donna's healing was not done and dusted at this pointed, but she had allowed the seeds of hope to take root in her heart and mind, which gave her a confident expectation that God was bringing her out of the illness into a place of emotional health and wholeness.

I can't thank Jay, Fiona and all the TC team enough for the grace and support that they showed me and Donna at that time. Despite living very busy lives, along with running a national charity with all its associated day-to-day responsibilities, they, and the team, still found it in their hearts to make just a little more room to help another person back to wholeness. Many talk about grace, but these people live it.

Donna and I then began the delicate process of getting our lives back on track. We had to take it slowly and thoughtfully. Most of the time I stayed at home to help out and tried to earn some money buying and selling stuff at auctions, to help reduce the financial strain we were under. Overall we began to laugh again as a family and just enjoyed being together again. Best of all, I had my wife back.

In the background, our discussions with Teen Challenge had been on going and not long after Donna's return home we made a family decision to move to the Midlands, so that Donna and I could work for TC. As part of their head office and men's centre relocation from South Wales to Leicestershire, they needed new staff and we had the privilege of being part of the team that helped move them to a fully refurbished, higher capacity home that now offers even more men the opportunity of finding true freedom from their destructive lifestyles.

We spent over a year working there and had a wonderful time partnering with an amazing organisation. Watching God transform the lives of many men who had arrived through the doors, dishevelled and gaunt from years of addiction, was an honour and a privilege.

The Locator

One summer's evening while we were living in

Leicestershire, the kids had gone to bed and we were sat in the living room enjoying a cuddle on the sofa when a programme came on the television that we had not planned to watch. The programme was called 'The Locator'. It was an American show presented by a host who acted on behalf of people who had given up their child for adoption many years beforehand. The TV host would then attempt to locate the child and ask if they would be open to a reunion with their birth parent. Inevitably, the show culminated in a reunion at the end of each show. It was a real tearjerker and brought to the surface in me, a whole host of emotions that had been buried deep within me for many years.

After watching the show over a few weeks, one night I said to Donna, "I may have another child, you know." A conversation followed between during which I told Donna all about the events of my teenage years. To my relief, she was brilliant about it all. I suppose knowing that I already had another child, Collette, before our marriage, coupled with her knowledge of my dysfunctional past, prevented the conversation being a total shock to her. The heart of compassion Donna showed upon receiving this news, brought great comfort to me. We talked into the early hours of the morning and discussed all possible outcomes, the doubts and questions, even the possibility that the child may not be mine. In my heart of hearts, I knew it was.

As a teenager, my initial response to discovering that I was a father, was one of denial and rejection, but the fact was, I knew it to be true. I had suppressed the truth under a tide of denial and drug taking. The heart never lies and even during my early years of drug use and dysfunction, every now and again a thought about my child would come into my mind at the most random of times and places. I always tried to ignore or reject it, or get so high I would forget about it. Another strange thing was that over the years my path had crossed with Tracey – the child's mum – at the most random of times. But each time I'd seen her, she hadn't seen me. There had never been any conversations or polite greetings, just a visible reminder to me of the mother and child I had once rejected.

Returning to our late night conversation on the sofa, Donna asked, "What are you going to do about it then?"

"I don't know," was my sullen reply.

"Well, if you do have another child, we will love him or her the same as the rest of the kids," she concluded.

I was astonished, snuggled up to her under the covers and held her tight. 'What an amazing wife I have,' was the last thought to run through my mind as I fell asleep.

I spent the next couple of weeks thinking over the possible outcomes. What if my child didn't want to know me? What if they did? Then what? And how do I go about trying to find them? What about my existing family, how would they feel about it? Then one evening after a particular episode of 'The Locator' had finished, Donna looked me square in the eyes and said in a very caring and loving tone, "If you want to try and find your child, I will be right by your side whatever the outcome." I took a deep breath in and told her that now I knew I had her full support, I would do it.

We put the kids to bed and started our journey in the only place we knew - Facebook. We sat in bed together and typed in the name of my friend from school and up came Tracey's profile. The first step was to submit a friend request. That done, there was no going back. I kid you not, but within no more than thirty seconds it was accepted. I was astounded. Next, I had to craft a message asking if I was the father of the child that she'd had as a teenager. I'd almost finished when Donna spotted I was about to post it publicly for all to see – whoops! So I did a rewrite and sent it as a private message. Lesson learned.

Those of you who know how Facebook works will know that as soon as the other person starts typing a reply, a little speech bubble appears so that you know it is on its way. My heart was in my mouth as I waited for what seemed like an eternity. Then up it popped. "YES, YES, YES you are," were its opening words, followed by others that I can't even remember; the yes was enough for me.

Donna sent a reply and introduced herself, and the two of them spent ages talking as if I didn't exist! Tracey had given birth to a boy - she had called Jon.

Tracey then sent us some photos. The first one, that I had never seen before, was of me aged fourteen with my brothers. Tracey had kept it, she explained, to give to her son if he ever came back into her life so he would know what his father looked like. The second photo was of the baby, no more than an hour old with a scrunched up face and chubby fingers, which Donna pointed out that he looked just like me – but just how that could be deduced from a picture like that is beyond the capacity of the male brain, I reckon; the third shot was of Jon aged about nine months.

Tracey shared with us that immediately after giving birth, the baby had been removed from the room for the normal checks, cleaning and dressing. The nurses had then taken a photograph and given the picture to her while the baby was moved to a private place in the hospital. He had then been placed in foster care until he was adopted by a loving couple who had no children of their own, when he was nine months old. The foster carers had taken the second photo just before his adoptive parents came to collect him and sent it to her.

At one point in the conversation Tracey asked me why I'd decided to contact her now, after all this time? I wasn't exactly sure how to answer but I'd already explained some of my story to her; so she knew I had been in a mess and was putting my life back together. All I could say was that I was now ready to take responsibility for my past and apologised for the fact that it had taken me so long to get to this point. She then stunned me by saying, "Well, I gave Jon up over twenty five years ago but after talking to my family about it, I decided to start the process of looking for him three weeks ago." Three weeks ago! I was amazed; it all seemed to be just falling into place.

As the evening and the facebook conversation wore on, my mind was filled with all kinds of emotions and long suppressed feelings, some of which I found hard to contain. Yet despite the emotional roller coaster I was experiencing, I felt very sure that everything was going to turn out all right. After an hour or so of messaging back and forth, we exchanged phone numbers so we could have a personal talk in a few days time once everything had sunk in.

How was I supposed to sleep after that? I kept looking at the two photos of my son and tried to imagine what he would look like today, aged twenty-five. Did he look like me? Did he have a family of his own? If he did, I could be a granddad! How had he done at school? What career path had he chosen? Hopefully not the one I'd chosen! And what if he is dead? You never know. But I just knew in my heart that he was alive and out there somewhere. Eventually, I drifted off for the most peaceful sleep I'd had for a long time.

I spoke to Tracey a few days later and arranged for us to travel up to meet her the following week. So within days, Donna and I were knocking on Tracey's front door. Donna hugged me tight and encouraged me with a smile, but inside I was so nervous – it must have shown.

Things went well and much to my relief, Tracey held no animosity towards me. The girls chatted like they were old friends and Tracey told us what information she had discovered to date in her search for Jon. She explained that there was a specialist government agency that helped birth parents to trace their adopted children and that should be our starting point. So we agreed to do it together and we left Tracey to make the appointment.

Our drive back home to the Midlands from Tracey's home in Wakefield was filled with a new sense of excitement. All we could talk about was the appointment with the agency and our hope that it would be soon. We were disappointed. It took months before we were finally given a date, which was at times, frustrating. I had to keep telling myself that I had waited over twenty-five years, so another few months wasn't going to kill me.

On the day of the appointment, Tracey and I were shown into a small office and offered a seat by a lady who then made herself comfortable in a chair that looked far more comfortable than the hard and creaky thing that I was sat on. She explained how the agency worked, then asked us both lots of questions, the main one being why we were now looking for the child. We then had opportunity to ask our questions - of which there were lots. I wanted to include asking her to swap chairs with me but decided against it. After an hour of intense and emotional conversation, we were all satisfied that we had enough information for the time being.

The next step was for the agency to make enquiries to establish if Jon was still alive and if so, to obtain a contact address. We would then be contacted and offered the opportunity to write him a letter, which the agency would forward on to him. Due to the fact that we were not in a relationship with each other, Tracey and I were advised to write separate letters when it came to it, and to meet him separately too – assuming of course that he was willing to see us. We were happy with these arrangements and the waiting game began. There was a lot of waiting - a frustrating amount. Three months passed before we were contacted again.

Dwain

Donna, Tracey and I kept in touch over the months until I eventually received the call I had been waiting for.

"They've found him!" Tracey's ecstatic shriek came as soon as I answered her call. "They've found him and said we can write to him," she continued excitedly, not letting me get a word in.

"Who, what, where and when?" were my equally excited responses. I was overjoyed and couldn't get my words out properly.

Once we had both regained our composure, Tracey explained that we could now write to Jon and the agency would forward our letters on to him. We were permitted to include any of our personal details so that he was then able to contact us directly should he wanted to take it any further.

"Wow!" Was all I could muster. "Wow!"

"Did they tell you anything more about him?," I pressed

Tracey, "is he well and does he have a family?" I tailed off.

"No, nothing at all", she said, "except that his parents chose to call him Dwain."

"Dwain?" I asked.

"But they did keep the name I gave him at birth as his middle name" she went on, "So he is Dwain Jon."

"That was kind of them", I replied.

We talked some more about who was going to write what and we decided that Tracey should write to him first and see how he responded before I wrote. I felt I owed Tracey that much, in that I'd been the one who had initially rejected the pair of them. I stepped aside momentarily to allow Tracey the freedom to walk the last leg of her journey with her own family. And so the first letter was sent.

While all this was going on, our time working for TC had come to an end. We felt it was the right time to move back to Yorkshire because of some family circumstances and we soon settled back into our family home, which we had rented out, whilst living in Leicestershire. I went back to work in the building trade and Donna started working for Christians Against Poverty, which she enjoyed immensely, and we eased back into family life

A few weeks later Tracey phoned and I heard her say the words I'd been longing to hear,

"I've just spoken to Dwain."

All lingering doubts about whether he would ever want to speak to either of us dissipated in a flash. She went on to tell me how he had first responded by letter, a couple of weeks after receiving hers. Then they had swapped telephone numbers and had been exchanging text messages for a week or so until Dwain chose to telephone her. That was the beginning of their relationship.

"Did he ask about me?" I asked, feeling a little selfish but I couldn't help myself.

"Yes he did," she answered confidently, and I have his email address for you to write to him which he would like you to do."

I was silent. I welled up inside and a tear trickled down my cheek as I tried to regain my composure.

"Thank you. Thank you so much," was about all I could mutter.

Later that evening, as I stared at the keyboard, hands shaking, I tried to think of how to start the most important letter of my life. Donna was by my side and slipped her hand around my waist and gave me a gentle squeeze, which was the source of strength that I needed to continue. "Just be you," she whispered to me.

I decided to keep the letter (or email) simple and introduced myself, the rest of the family and enquired after him and his family. I left it at that, not forgetting to include my phone number. I hit send, completing one more tentative step on my journey of restoration.

The 22nd April 2013 was like any other ordinary day in the life of our family; getting the kids to eat their breakfast and out to school on time; going to work; returning just as tea was put on the table; spending a couple of hours trying to stop the kids fighting over the remote control; getting their homework done; putting pyjamas on (whilst never taking their eyes off of the television screen) and finally going to bed. That evening I had flopped down in the chair and was flicking through the TV channels to see if there was any football on, when my phone rang.

"Hello" I said, a tinge disappointingly having just discovered there were no live matches on.

The voice at the other end of the line simply said, "Hello Tim, it's Dwain."

Complete

I wasn't shocked or lost for words, after all, the last nine months of my life had been leading up to that point and I was ready for it. "Hello Dwain, how are you?" I simply replied. We talked for the next ten minutes or so before the call had to be cut short owing to the fact that Dwain needed to respond to an emergency call he had just received – he was a paramedic. That was the simplicity of how our relationship began.

I was elated when I got off of the phone and waited excitedly for Donna to come into the room to tell her that I had just had my first conversation with Dwain.

"How, when?" was her confused response.

"Just now - he rang me up." I continued, and I filled Donna in with the contents of the brief conversation I'd had with Dwain, which she wasn't content with. Donna wanted more information as only women do.

"Did you laugh? Did you cry? Did you get emotional?" She probed.

"No" was my short reply.

We had been two adults talking, so there weren't any tears just lots of questions and answers, with a few laughs and suppressed emotions along the way. Dwain and I continued to talk regularly over the next couple of weeks and finally arranged to meet one Sunday morning.

We met at the local coffee shop, bought some drinks, made ourselves comfortable on some outside chairs, and spent the next two hours talking and getting to know one another under the beautiful morning sunshine. I told him all about my past, which I hoped would in some way help him to understand my life situation at the time of his birth and reiterated that he had never been far from my thoughts over the years. He was fantastic with me and assured me that he didn't hold anything against me. He'd had a fantastic upbringing by wonderful, loving parents who had, incidentally, told Dwain that he was adopted at quite a young age. It hadn't come as a total surprise when Tracey's letter arrived.

Many people have since asked me how I felt during that first meeting with Dwain - was I nervous? Was it strange or a shock in any way? My simple answer is - no. After all, this was my son and despite the obvious gap of twenty-five years, I felt comfortable with him and totally at ease, like I would with any of my children; except he wasn't a child, he was a fully-grown man. My feelings towards him were just the same as all of my children.

Just in case you are wondering - yes, he does look like me – but without the ginger Afro! He has the Haigh family eyes and other features from my mum's side of the family. In fact I have a cousin on mum's side of the family, not much older than Dwain who is the double of him - no need for a DNA test on that point!

After that first meeting we arranged for him to come and meet the rest of the family. It was amazing to see him arrive at the house a few weeks later. He walked in with an air of confidence that reminded me a lot of myself and put everyone at ease. Jack and Chloe loved the fact that they had an older brother and just wanted to play games with him and clamber all over him. Collette was also present and, despite the fact that she was no longer the eldest child in the family, she also enjoyed meeting her new older brother.

One of the big questions I asked Dwain was whether he was a parent himself. I was delighted to discover he had two boys aged six and one – I was a granddad! What amuses me is that at the time Chloe was almost six and Jack three, so I have a biological grandson who is older than my two youngest children. Just another page in the life of Tim Haigh!

That first meeting took place over two years ago and Dwain and I have remained in constant touch ever since. We've enjoyed some great times together, especially around Christmases and birthdays. It turns out that Dwain and I were born just a week apart, so we try to arrange a joint party for the both of us during the week between our birthdays. The first time we did it, we arranged for Tracey to join us and bring her two children, and so Dwain had all his siblings with him for the first time, which made for a great evening and some even better photographs. Before we contacted him, Dwain had been an only child. Overnight he had found out that he had five brothers and sisters, something he always jokes about at Christmas, which now costs him a small fortune! Happy days.

I close with one special memory. On the first visit Dwain made to our home, over two years ago, we had spent such a great evening together, chatting, laughing, taking photographs and asking lots of questions; just getting to know one another. Then at one stage in the evening I left the room for something. As I walked back into the room from the kitchen, I stood in the doorway and took a moment to look upon my whole family, all together for the first time. From deep within me rose a sense that at last I was complete. I smiled to myself and re-joined my family, my whole family.

11

Changed

IT is now over seventeen years since I had that life-transforming encounter with Jesus. And before signing off, let me take a moment to bring you up to date with what my life looks like today.

I am still married to the lovely Donna and we live in a delightful converted barn in a rural part of Yorkshire with our two children, Chloe who is now eight and Jack who is five. Collette, my eldest daughter has a great job in the city of Leeds and has just moved out of her mum's house into her first new flat. She is now twenty-two, is caring, compassionate, and so very beautiful, even if I am rather biased.

And what about my old friends who fell in to the trap of addiction? Sadly many of them have died through overdoses or other causes associated with their lifestyle. I know of some who managed to get free from their heroin addiction, only to return to it later, then get free again, then return; an on-off cycle that is slowly killing them. Others friends of mine have managed to get clean from the heroin, only to substitute it with another intoxicant like prescribed opium substitutes, alcohol or dope. I can say with all honesty that I only know of a handful of people who have come off heroin and managed to live completely free from it for a good number of years. These statistics make me very sad and are testament to the destructive, life-dominating power of hard drugs.

Looking ahead

Now what? I have lots of life still to live and a growing sense of what God wants me to do for him in the next season of my life.

Since I completed the Teen Challenge programme, over sixteen years ago, I have always held a deep passion for sharing my story, as a way of encouraging and helping others. I believe that if God can change my life he can change theirs too. I have taken every opportunity to do so and I guess this book is just another expression of that passion.

My willingness to share my story has taken me into churches, schools and aid agencies all over the UK. I just tell it as it is, exactly as you have read in these pages, and always with a view to connecting people with Jesus, the only true answer. I have even had the privilege of writing articles for newspapers and have appeared on two television programmes, all the time, telling my story of moving from addiction to freedom.

The most exciting opportunity came my way over ten years ago, when I received my first invitation to speak at a prison chapel service. The chaplain had heard my story somehow and thought it would be great for the young adults in the young offenders prison (secure college of learning is the politically correct term) to hear a real life story from someone who had once been in prison, lived a life of drug addiction and then found freedom from it through faith in Jesus Christ.

As soon as I walked through the gates of that young offender's prison, I knew it was where I belonged, not serving time as a prisoner but as a messenger of hope. I poured out my heart to the young men during that chapel service and the room fell silent as they listened intently to my message of hope. I could literally see the hope beginning to rise in their hearts; they began to sit more uprightly in their chairs and lean into what I was saying. It was in those moments that I felt as if God was smiling as I told my story. From that moment I started to believe that my former pain could now be used to help many others navigate theirs and find the route to freedom in Christ.

The responses from the young lads at the end of the service were very positive which I found uplifting and a further confirmation that I must continue doing what I had done that day. That was the start of the prison ministry I still do today and which I intend to develop further over the coming months and years.

In the months that followed that first prison chapel service, I had the opportunity to go back and speak again. As I continued to pray about my future and how best to use my story to help others, God began to open doors for me to speak in other prisons in the Yorkshire district and one prison in particular – Armley Prison in Leeds. How amazing is that? I had once determined never to set foot in the place again but I was wrong, I attend the chapel services regularly and am a voice of hope against the darkness.

The increasing numbers of visits to speak in, what were higher security establishments, required me to gain special security clearance from the authorities. I completed all the necessary paperwork and sent off for my CRB (Criminal

Records Bureau) check, which formed part of the application process. When it finally arrived, I had to laugh - it was four pages long, full of my criminal record. I then took it and the other paper work to the prison where my security clearance application was being processed, the officer receiving the application had a quick look through to make sure all the relevant forms were there, then laughed out loud when she got to my CRB form.

"They will never give you clearance with a record like this," she confidently stated.

"I have seen them refuse clearance for people with only a fraction of the charges you have," she finished. I just smiled, thanked her for handling the application process and left the office.

As I walked across the prison car park, I said this simple prayer: "Father God, if you want me to serve you in the prison system, then I trust you to arrange my clearance." It was that short and simple.

My simple faith was rewarded, to the surprise of many officers at the prison. I received a full security clearance and thereby gained the freedom to continue bringing my message of hope into men's, women's and young offenders prisons in the North of England. God is a God of the impossible!

Now, instead of supplying heroin and causing pain and anguish to people, I now supply hope and freedom, using my life story as the example and proof that God is real. If he can do it for me, he can do it for anyone. God desires to transform every broken life into a whole and healthy one, where a person is willing to give their life to Jesus and allow him to love them unconditionally.

Thank you for reading my story. I pray that God uses it

to inspire those of you who are suffering to press through your personal pain into freedom and liberty as I have done. I also pray it will encourage you to tell your story, because just as many that have been, and will be helped by mine, there are others who will need to hear your story of how our great and loving God specialises in healing the broken and leading them into freedom.

Like me, you cannot change your past – but you can change its meaning. A leopard can change its spots.

'Jesus provided far more God-revealing signs than are written down in this book. These are written down so you will believe that Jesus is the Messiah, the Son of God, and in the act of believing, have real and eternal life in the way he personally revealed it.'

(John 20:30-31, The Message Bible)

My Invitation

So, you have made it to the end of this book and there's a good chance you have been on a personal journey of emotional highs and lows along the way. You may have laughed or cried in one paragraph, then been shocked or astonished in the next. However you'd describe your experience, I'm pretty sure you're at the very least intrigued; intrigued about the validity of my life story and intrigued about this loving God who I talk so openly about. My response to your intrigue is to extend a personal invitation to you.

First, permit me to preface my invitation with a couple of comments. Firstly about the God I have spoken so enthusiastically about: He is not an angry and condemning God. Neither is he looking at people's lives with a view to causing them pain and misery, which unfortunately is the way he has been represented by some people. I simply ask you to lay aside any negative, preconceived ideas you may have about God, and open your heart to the truth that he loves and adores you completely. He longs for you to just come to him as you are, which has been made possible by Jesus Christ, and for you to abide with him for all eternity.

If you read the Bible carefully and in the way God intended, you will see that it is a love story, the greatest love story ever told. It is the story of a God who was separated from those he loved through no fault of his own, yet he stopped at nothing until he had made a way for those he loved to be reconciled with him again. And you are one of those he loves. Yes you.

The Bible paints a beautiful picture of a 'marriage proposal', one that God extends to every person alive. He effectively offers you his hand in marriage. The question simply becomes, will you accept God's personal proposal to you? When you accept God's offer, you will be gifted forgiveness of every bad thing you have ever done (what the Bible calls 'sin'). You will experience peace, hope and joy in your heart and I promise you that you will never be the same person again.

God does not want you to go through life feeling alone and unloved, weighed down by guilt and condemnation from things you have done, or not done, in your life. He wants you to know that he loves you unconditionally right where you are today – yes, right now. And all you have to do to embrace a future beyond your wildest dreams is simply accept his hand of proposal.

That is the invitation that I extend to you today: to accept the invitation God is extending to you.

Will you accept God's proposal?

If you are saying "yes" to this question, let me lead you in a conversation that you can have with God right now. Don't delay. Say this out loud and mean it from your heart:

Father God I accept your proposal.
I admit I have done and said things in my life
that have caused a separation between us.
I admit my sin and I ask you, Lord Jesus,
to forgive me.

I receive your forgiveness and thank you for it.
And I ask you, Father God, to fill my heart and life with
your perfect love which you have promised
to freely give me.

I now choose to live my life walking with you and
depending on your love for me.

Amen.

If you have just said this prayer and accepted God's offer of salvation, I salute and honour you.

So "what now?" I hear you thinking. Well I think it's important that you tell someone about the decision you have just made and then find yourself a good local church where you can find a Christian family you can become a part of; a place to belong. If you are currently in prison, then contact the chaplaincy team there and join in the Sunday or mid week meetings.

Please feel free to contact me and tell me about the decision you have just made. It would make my day! And if you have any difficulties finding a local church, do also feel free to contact me or one of my team and we will help you find a good one that you will be able to call home.

This Book and the Future

A T the outset of this book I explained my reasons for writing it. But now what? Well, I have some hopes and dreams for its future use, which I'd love to share with you.

My big dream is to make this book freely available to every person currently held within the UK prison system. At the time of writing – early 2016 – that's more than 85,000 people held in over 130 prisons and young offender units.

Every one of those prisoners is someone's son or daughter and many are also mothers or fathers themselves. They each have a relational world that has been devastated by their incarceration, meaning the ripple affect of their crime and punishment is massive when you multiply it out. Countless thousands of people are involved in supporting a loved one in prison or have been affected negatively because of their sentence. My heart aches for them, particularly the children innocently caught up in the destructive after-effects of crime.

Many of them will resonate with my story, maybe not every aspect of it but certainly with enough for it to potentially be a beacon of hope in the darkness they are experiencing. I want people who are in prison or caught up in addictions to know that there is a better life they can aspire to, a life that is within touching distance if they make the right determined choices today. And reading this book could be the starting point of that change.

You can help make this dream a reality. I will do all I can but that's always going to be limited in its overall impact if I try to do it all myself, which is why I would greatly value your partnership in the work, either as a business, church, charitable organization or simply as an individual. Together we can make the dream a reality!

The simplest way to help is by sponsoring the printing and distribution of this book, thus enabling us to give free copies to those in greatest need. Beyond that, we have other initiatives in the pipeline involving its distribution in colleges, police stations, detention centres, immigration holding units and other related charities.

Will you help us?

If you would like to help and support our work, please don't hesitate to contact me – Tim Haigh – email *hello@timhaigh.net*

All donations and book sponsorships are processed through my governing charity, 'Fathers Heart Ministries', UK charity number 1069817 and are not received by me personally.

Contact

If you would like to contact me for any reason , please use any of the details listed below

www.timhaigh.net.
Email *hello@timhaigh.net*
Facebook *Tim Haigh*

If you would like to book Tim to speak and share his story at a mission, event or conference you are hosting, then please email us with your request and dates.

If you would like to order further copies of this book or would like to know more about the ministry work in prisons that Tim does, then please visit our website.

Should you require any further information about the Teen Challenge rehabilitation centre, then please contact them through any of the listed information on the page overleaf.

It is the mission of Teen Challenge to to provide men, women and young adults with an effective and comprehensive faith-based solution to drug and alcohol addiction as well as other life controlling problems.

Teen Challenge
Willoughby house
Station road
Upper Broughton
Melton Mowbray.
Leicestershire.
LE14 3BH

01664 822221
Email   info@teenchallenge.org.uk
www.teenchallenge.org.uk
Registered UK charity no 298900.